CASES IN PUBLIC MANAGEMENT

D0140857

CASES IN PUBLIC MANAGEMENT

FIFTH EDITION

EDITED BY

Robert T. Golembiewski
University of Georgia

Jerry G. Stevenson
University of Arkansas at Little Rock

Michael White
University of Southern California

F.E. PEACOCK PUBLISHERS, INC.
Itasca, Illinois

Acknowledgments

A grateful acknowledgment is due those whose names appear in the *Casebook Contributors* list, which follows. Many of the cases are provided by our friends, students, and colleagues in public management. And several individuals who provided cases or information prefer to remain unidentified, but their contributions are gratefully, if anonymously, acknowledged.

Special thanks to our respective life partners and families whose patience, love, and encouragement are critical to endeavors of this sort. The staff and graduate assistants at the University of Arkansas at Little Rock's Institute of Government—Philis Cooper, Robin Wilson, Kim Jackson, Cindy Boland, and Terry Mobley—provided excellent assistance in preparing this volume for publication.

Advisory Editor in Public Administration
Bernard H. Ross
School of Public Affairs
American University

Contents

Casebook Contributors   vii
Introduction   1
Table A-1. Classification of Cases by Managerial Issues   15

PART ONE
Bargaining and Negotiations
1. A Tiger in the Planning Section   21
2. ACLU v. Tyler County   24
3. Budget Cuts   30
4. Commercial Free Speech?   32
5. Intransigence and Inertia   35
6. Middle Management Ignored   41
7. Who Staffs the Hospital?   46

PART TWO
Ethical and Personal Dilemmas
8. A Zealous City Employee   53
9. AIDS Patients   58
10. Ann's Dilemma   60
11. A Case of Bureaucratic Morality?   63
12. Anna Lieberman, Deceased   65
13. One Perspective on Hillsdale Tower   70
14. The Outsider   78
15. Thompson's Time Management   82

PART THREE
Organizational and Leadership Issues
16. Agency Capture?   89
17. Deliah's In-Basket   90
18. Dilemma in Juvenile Court   96
19. Effective Leadership?   104

20. Going to the Dogs!   106
21. Hail to the New Chief   109
22. Shifting the Costs of Governance   112

PART FOUR
Organizational Change and Culture
23. A License for Quality: TQM at the BMV   119
24. Doing Hard Time: Reforming the Prison System   125
25. Environmental Quality   128
26. Mixed Effects of a Demonstration Project   129

PART FIVE
Personnel and Human Resource Issues
27. A Supervisor for Unit II   141
28. Affirmative Action in Hamilton County   144
29. HIV and Employee Rights   150
30. Performance Evaluation and Organizational Rigidity   153
31. The Police Captain Dilemma   158
32. Reasonable Accommodation   160
33. A Subordinate's Homophobia   163

PART SIX
Policies and Procedures
34. A Matter of Evaluation   169
35. Annual Daffodil Festival   172
36. Metropolitan Emergency Medical Services   174
37. Of Bounded Cooperation   179
38. The *Challenger* Shuttle Disaster   184
39. The Gesture That Went Awry   189

PART SEVEN
Supervisory Problems
40. An Office Romance   193
41. Carl the Ripper   197
42. Conflicts on the Human Services Coordination Team   200
43. The Making of a Corrections Officer   207
44. Distributing County Property Without Consent   213
45. Easing Toward Change in Urbania's Finance Department   215
46. "Keep a Two-by-Four Behind Your Desk"   220
47. "Stop Having Birthdays!"   224
48. One Supervisor's Analysis   229

Index   233

Casebook Contributors

Thomas E. Allen, Jr.
David B. Amick
Francis P. Anzelmi
Steven H. Appelbaum
Richard M. Ayres
Elaine Baker
J. Norman Baldwin
Darold T. Barnum
Raymond G. Beck
Wendell Broadwell
David S. Brown
Edward Brown, Jr.
Scott B. Button
Thomas G. Butts
Bonnie L. Clark
Ross Clayton
Robert W. Cole
Debbie Cutchin
J. Shannon Davis
Bryan Day
John Ellis
Marilyn Farley
Charles W. Fleming
Asa B. Foster, Jr.
Charles N. Fowler
Ronald Fraser

Steven B. Frates
Bruce Fusner
William C. Gaines
Vickie Gates
John Gehl
Horst B. Glatte
Robert T. Golembiewski
Timothy J. Grogg
George E. Hale
Meredith Anne Hart
Robert C. Helt
Patrick Henningan
Bob M. Inge
Robert G. Johnson
Gwendolyn L. Jones
Robert Kershaw
Jonathan Kleinwarks
Mark Kohntopp
Robert S. LaSala
Edward Anthony Lehan
Jeff T. Lewis
John Maples
Anthony R. Marchione
Albert R. Martin
David Mason
Richard Mays

Alan McClain
Francis P. McGee
Maureen M. McIntosh
Joseph A. Mitchell
Robin Mullin
Robert Murtagh
Gopal Pati
Harry G. Perkins
Donald R. Peterson
Ernest Powell, Jr.
Dewey Price
Gerard J. Quinn
John H. Rheinscheld
Wilber C. Rich
Dorothy Jane Riggs
Matthews J. Robbins
Roby D. Robertson
Philip Rosenberg
Richard D. Schmitt

Bob Schultz
G. W. Sheldon
Gordon M. Sherman
Frank R. Shults
Lawrence L. Singer
David W. Sink
Patricia Somers
Jane Freeman Steagall
Eldon Steeves
Jerry G. Stevenson
Joe C. Strange
Ronald E. Usher
Stuart Vexler
Eugene W. Washington
Thomas L. Wheelen
Michael White
Steven C. Wilkins
Roger Williamson
James Winship

Introduction

SOME CHARACTERISTICS OF MANAGERIALLY RELEVANT CASES

Managerially relevant cases have a distinctive character and purpose. All cases in this volume deal with a problem or situation that has existed or now exists in some public organization. The problem or situation typically involves decisions previously made, or a decision that needs making, and each requires analysis, which offers students an opportunity to learn from another's experience and engage in constructive second-guessing.

Criteria for Cases

Each problem or situation must meet four conditions for selection in this casebook. *First*, cases must be both credible and manageable. Each case narrative seeks to be realistic while avoiding encumbering detail. Sufficient data are provided—both directly and by implication—to generate analysis and discussion related to a specific managerial situation.

Second, the aggregate collection of case studies must suggest the range of phenomena typically encountered by a public manager. Overall, the collection should reflect the impact of characteristic institutions, issues, and traditions of public employment. These processes and dynamics cover a wide range: the causes and effects of managerial actions; the motivation and morale of employees; the structure and policies that define a work site; the consequences of specific managerial styles; the interaction of program analysis and program politics; the effects of performance measures or financial controls on individual and group behavior; and other intended and unintended factors in organizational life.

Third, each case study seeks to heighten interest and increase involvement and awareness by raising significant issues that managers might face. The cases also suggest ways to respond and are intended to increase the reader's sense of mastery over what he or she may confront in managerial life.

Fourth, on balance, the cases should emphasize *praxis*, which the dictionary defines as "the exercise or practice of an art, science, or skill." This skill-practice can be mental, as the prepared mind develops a mode for search for the relevant details. The practice also can involve consciously building an inventory of possible responses to managerial situations, along with reasonably anticipated consequences. And the skill-practice can focus on the use of specific tools and concepts. For example, some cases would profit from a needs assessment, others from strategic planning, and so on.

Given such descriptive complexities, this volume seeks to encourage reflection and searching by the learner. The case approach attempts to develop the ability to suspend judgment, to "dangle," while data are being gathered and the mind's complex processes are at work isolating, assimilating, and integrating the multiple cues triggered by the case. This suspension of judgment must be coupled with aggressive efforts at observation and search, but inducing this combination is seldom a simple or direct matter. Commonly, learners develop—even leap to— premature judgments and evaluations about some action sequence, and settle matters by short-circuiting the required analysis.

Learning to suspend judgment until analysis is advanced can be very useful for the superviser or manager. By using the case method, one can develop this skill without first making mistakes in some actual managerial context. A typical case presents both "good" and "bad" managerial practices and policies, without identifying either, and no case stands as a measure of effective or ineffective managerial behavior or policy. The reader can make such judgments but should reserve them for later. The intent is detailed analysis more than evaluation, especially premature evaluation. The goal is not to present specific "right ways" but rather to help people learn habits for analysis—involving processes, attitudes, and skills—that will increase the probability of effective public management.

But the case method has other goals—to stimulate the development of insight, the testing of knowledge, and the enrichment of analytical skills.

In the classroom situation, the case approach places the responsibility for learning on the student, and discussion is the prime vehicle by which participants expand their own skills and resources. This makes it imperative that the student carefully read and review each case prior to its presentation.

Analyses and discussions of cases are likely to be richest and most provocative when they involve participants who have one or both of two attributes: substantial organizational experience, or command of frames of reference or models that guide observation and analysis. These can help enrich case analysis and discussion. Short lectures by a resource person can add to a learner's repertoire of models or perspectives relevant to work and its management. Broad and detailed reading in the various behavioral science literature is also helpful.

Advantages of Case Method

The case method has a number of other significant advantages. Consider the immediate relevance of the subject matter to the learner. This relevance will help enhance skills in analysis and synthesis as well as cultivate the ability to separate the significant from the trivial in the world of administrative reality. Perhaps the most direct route to enhancing observation, analysis, and synthesis is through the learner's development of three kinds of interacting repertoires:

- Interactions that direct attention to significant administrative data or to the lack thereof.
- Models or theories that tie together discrete observations or that permit implications of the form: Since I have observed x, I should be careful to check for z and w, which often co-vary with x.
- Alternative actions, whose variations are increasingly elaborated and tested.

To put it briefly, using the case approach should increase one's ability to isolate problems and develop solutions. This doesn't promise that case users will learn how to solve problems without creating others. Far from it. But case analysis should sensitize the user to some of the more obvious issues and traps involved in managerial problem solving, and alert the user to a growing sense of the consequences of specific actions or decisions.

Also, the case method is built around significant managerial processes that communicate to others an analysis or program of action in a way that encourages understanding, induces minimal defensiveness on the part of others, and provides some motivational leverage when and if the time comes to act. Even if the analysis is brilliant and the program an absolute gem, these managerial processes will be of use in both the classroom and the public agency. No public manager can have too much experience with these critical processes. Indeed, many have too little.

Case studies also help facilitate the transfer of learning from the classroom to the work site, a critical step in the learning process. This transfer will become increasingly probable as:

- learners come to know their own work-related attitudes and values,
- they learn to define classes of more or less typical situations, and
- they develop broader repertoires for analysis and greater awareness of the probable consequences of various responses to managerial situations.

The case approach emphasizes meeting only those three conditions. Transfer can also be enhanced by the apt teacher or resource person who helps frame or guide the discussion of a case with relevant theory and penetrating questions for discussion.

KINDS OF LEARNING AND THE CASE APPROACH

A simple review of five kinds of learning promoted by the case-study method may further clarify the special niche of the managerially relevant case. *First*, these cases are not used primarily to *transmit knowledge*, though some transmission will naturally occur. Cases provide pictures or images of real problems and real situations, which provide the learner with knowledge of, or insight about, what is likely to be encountered in an organization. Case discussions can be potent vehicles for sharing perspectives and insights.

Second, managerially relevant cases are more likely to facilitate the *integration* or *application of knowledge*. The case method builds on the experiences of others by adding to a learner's experiential memory bank in a convenient and economical way. The case is packaged and simplified reality, through which knowledge of general principles or regularities can be integrated into analyses and tested against case-study reality to help establish both the usefulness and limitations of particular knowledge. Most important, cases underscore the need for general principles or regularities, which can provide a powerful impetus to aggressive learning. These often are supplied by the behavioral sciences. Case studies can also help spotlight areas where reliable generalizations are unavailable.

Third, the case-study method reflects the approach's essential goal of contributing to the development by the learner of increasingly sophisticated and useful *mental sets* or *problem-solving postures*. These demonstrate that managerial situations are in part analyzable, though complex. At their developed best, they provide the individual with ways to isolate and deal with managerial realities that are both useful and consistent with the needs and evolving character of the individual. These sets or postures are important components of a person's "style," of his or her fundamental and characteristic ways of approaching and dealing with managerial problems. This style is highly individualistic and cannot evolve merely through processes of direct knowledge transmission. Such transmission can help or misguide the development of such sets and postures.

Fourth, learning via the case study emphasizes the *examination of attitudes and values*. Here, the basic dynamic is interpersonal. The individual reflects his or her attitudes, values, or managerial orientations, which are then confronted, supported, or jostled by the attitudes/values/orientation of other learners. The results of this interactive learning are difficult to predict or test, in contrast to the transmission of knowledge. There is no easy road to correct answers about issues of value or attitude.

The results of this fourth kind of learning can take many forms. Most commonly, mutual comparison and testing result in mutual insight and incorporation of some observations from the other learners into one's own expanding set of attitudes. Various new or modified attitudes can emerge, which lead to succeeding rounds of comparison and testing. The new or modified products can ossify, or they can continually evolve and become transmuted in subtle ways as the individual develops more detailed maps of his or her administrative territory. Alternatively, the individual learner may clash with others and choose to retain certain attitudes or values, a reaction that is neither stubborn nor heroic. But if the case approach is used appropriately, it should indicate to learners some specific sense of the costs and benefits of retaining their set of attitudes, values, or orientations, if that is what they choose to do.

Fifth, cases are very useful in the *synergistic sense of enlarging the repertoire of attitudes and skills that learners can use to approach values they feel are desirable*. This point is an important consequence of combining the two previous emphases.

ADVANTAGES OF THE CASE APPROACH: A REPRISE

Case studies provide an opportunity to test out and acquire a set of actions and behaviors that will permit some "enrichment of means," if only vicariously and verbally, at first. There is nothing like the firing line, of course. But case studies do provide a useful first stage for converting what Argyris calls "espoused theories" into "theories-in-use." Experience, or "having been there before," is usually a major factor in effective performance, and case studies provide an economic way of "having been there." As these comments suggest, the case approach:

- Emphasizes the identification of problems in managerially relevant situations like those that learners will experience at work.
- Reduces resistance to learning and increases involvement.
- Exposes learners to discussions that encompass different approaches, interpretations, and personalities.
- Helps expand the analytical focus and problem-solving orientations of learners, especially those with a compartmentalized view of organizations, or those with "tunnel vision."
- Permits the relatively safe testing of analyses and action proposals, a kind of learning less likely to occur under the pressure of work, where rigidity and defensiveness are more probable than searching introspection.
- Facilitates what might be called learning by empathy, as the learners identify with persons in a case or succeed in placing themselves in various roles or situations.
- Reduces the depersonalization and abstraction associated with much teaching and learning, which alienate many learners.
- Has a high claim to "relevance" and helps provide motivation to master behavioral science data for integration and application in analyses.

This casebook seeks to capitalize on these advantages to enrich the education and training of public administrators, and we editors see the cases as broadly useful for a wide variety of learners. The advantages just discussed relate to most of us, most of the time. Not that any one case fits everyone's learning needs, but this casebook does provide a range of cases that can be tailored to many learning/teaching environments and needs.

THE PRESENT CASES IN PUBLIC MANAGEMENT

The cases in this volume have a past as well as a present, as it were. That is, about 40 percent come from earlier versions of the casebook.

These are oldies but goodies, to put the point in show-business terms. All of the cases seek to meet three requirements for a teaching and learning resource useful in public administration courses and programs.

First, they encourage attention to the kind of clashes or incompatibilities that typically develop between the demands of a career in public administration and the needs, attitudes, ambitions, and values of the public official. In short, the cases encourage more attention to "in here" phenomena than to those "out there."

Second, these managerially oriented cases emphasize issues at the first level of supervision and at middle management, levels that generally deal with overseeing employees and directing of managers, respectively. Executive-level concerns—that is, those concerns directly associated with developing and maintaining a large enterprise—get little attention. Note, however, that even executives will find that many issues and processes in the cases are familiar, not only from their experience but also from their day-to-day activities. The familiar issues and processes include the responses of others to styles of management, executive preferences for search behavior and problem solving, and the ethical and moral dilemmas often encountered in managerial work at all levels.

Third, the cases—even those with an analytical focus—were chosen to provide showcases for various applications to the behavioral sciences, to generate numerous opportunities for integration of diverse behavioral science findings and perspectives.

This volume presents 48 cases that can contribute to diverse learning goals in various ways. In effect, the cases provide a simulated "here and now" into which readers can project themselves, as present-tense learners. The purpose is to expand one's portfolio of perspectives and approaches that may later be applied in "action scans" of working environments so as to enrich analysis and inform choice making.

Some Common Focal Concerns

Following this Introduction, Table A-1 lists for each case a number of behavioral science and public-management issues that can be highlighted in group discussion and with supplemental readings. Users will each have their own sense of what readings and behavioral science findings or perspectives will best help isolate or describe the dynamics of each of the cases to follow. These users include both teachers and students, whose roles are not always distinct and unchanging in the analysis and discussion of case studies. The ideal is interactive learning, in which occupants of both roles contribute and receive.

Usually, the application and integration of behavioral sciences relate to a case study as the general rule relates to the specific incident. The case serves as a specific reality base against which complex comparisons with behavioral science knowledge or theory can be made, with the goal of enriching the analysis of administrative life. Theory and knowledge can also suggest insights about alternative courses of action that enlarge the response repertoires of administrators-in-training.

Table A-1 classifies the cases in terms of the major managerial concerns and issues they highlight. This cataloging may help readers plan their use of this volume. The editors' purpose was to explicitly test the coverage of this collection. The typical case will imply several major focal concerns or issues. The breadth of coverage is suggested by the fact that the table distinguishes 18 focal concerns and managerially relevant issues. These are not exhaustive or exclusive; the collection does not cover every important topic in public management. In future editions we shall seek to address significant shifting of emphasis that changing conditions or helpful users bring to our attention.

Safe Contexts for Simulated Analysis and Action

Each case study seeks to provide an opportunity for some simulated analysis-cum-action. The general philosophy is that at least some useful learning can occur, even though the individual is not responsible for success or failure in the same sense as at work. To be sure, the case approach does not safeguard the learner from all risk of failure or censure, for fellow discussants can be both challenging and demanding of case analyses or proposals for action. But it does give the learner some sense of the visceral experiences and anxieties associated with supervision and management.

The goal of simulating analysis-cum-action is approached this way. Typically, the leaner is asked to assume a specific role with respect to the details of a case study and to develop analyses and proposals for action that can be discussed and variously tested. For example, one case may deal with a troublesome employee. Directions in the case study may ask the reader to assume the role of the employee's supervisor—which will allow the learner to react to the case narrative and analyze its dynamics with the help of whatever experience or information or models of reality he or she has. Thus the learner may develop an action program to achieve some supervisory goals in the specific context of the case.

The orienting directions for the learner usually are given at the end of a case narrative. This varies when a case has more than one part.

PREPARING CASES FOR CLASSROOM AND TRAINING USE

Effective use of the cases in this book requires careful planning. This preparation has two parts—substance and process. *Substance* refers to choosing which issues to emphasize through the *process* techniques chosen. *Process* refers to techniques for using the case in class assignments, group configurations, role playing, and projective methods.

Preparation of Case Substance

The following is a four-step method for identifying and choosing the issues raised by an individual case. This method allows each instructor (or student) to formulate an individual perspective on the content of a case.

Step One

To analyze the content or substance of a case, read it through a couple of times. As you read, jot down the issues being raised by the characters, situations, and events. Table A-1 gives some examples.

Step Two

Compare your issues with those in our list. Peruse the list and see if you want to add to, subtract from, or modify it. Don't concentrate on how we have classified the case. The purpose of this step is simply to help you consider a full range of issues.

After reviewing the issues in the table, you should have a revised list. This will reflect your own experience, education, and personality. There is no "correct" or "incorrect" list—only an organization that allows you to use the case with more or less effectiveness for your own course or training objectives.

Step Three

Begin a dialogue with our classifications for the case. Turning to an individual case, compare the list of issues you have prepared in the first two steps with the issues we have checked off for the same case. You may feel comfortable with the differences or may, after asking yourself "Why have they classified the case in this way?" gain new insight into the possibilities offered by the case. Then make a final list of issues you want to emphasize in class discussion and student assignments.

Step Four

Finally, scan your library and memory as well as the class or training readings. Seek articles, books, or reports that offer pertinent empirical findings, theories, or narratives for the issues you choose to emphasize. Then you will have the substance of the case prepared in some depth. This will help you choose techniques for using the case on the basis of well-thought-out, substantive learning objectives. The table, which represents our individual backgrounds, should reduce the amount of time it takes to prepare the substantive discussion. Once the case has been reviewed and evaluated in this manner, you can easily refresh your preparation from your notes.

Linkages With Selected Readings

Carefully selected readings will enrich and focus the learning potential of cases and do not need to be matched one-to-one, but can be linked one-to-several or several-to-several. Generally, useful reading assignments are abundantly available in other books and journals and, once an instructor has given some thought to these cases, relevant readings will readily come to mind. The same cases can be used for different purposes with different readings. Although they have been grouped under seven topical headings, all are sufficiently rich to allow for alternative topical focus.

We believe that both students and instructors can benefit from the four-step method presented in this section. Instructors might find this method helpful in motivating students to search the journal literature of public administration and the behavioral sciences.

Preparation of Cases for Discussion

The number of ways of using cases in the classroom approaches the number of instructors using them. Each instructor has an individual style; each case offers several possibilities; each course or course unit has specific objectives. In preparing a case for classroom use the instructor must consider his or her objectives and personal style as well as the possibilities offered by the case.

The reader knows more than we do about his or her own style. Do you prefer technical or intuitive approaches? Are you comfortable with conflict among your students or between yourself and the class? Do you like to lead the class toward specific insights or let it grope toward its own discovery? Do you like to create uncertainty and raise questions, or do you have clear and specific course objectives? Each user of this casebook should consider these questions and develop an overall strategy for the use of cases in the context of a specific course and social setting.

Cases themselves constrain their use. Some pose ethical problems; some pose interpersonal problems; some call for the design of behavioral interventions; some demand hard analysis. The instructor must assess the constraints of the case to determine its use. Another dimension imposed is the kind of social arrangements the case permits. Some cases lend themselves to role playing. Students or trainees can play the characters in the case directly. Several cases emphasize dialog between characters, while others allow each student to compose a written memorandum, and still others encourage a formal in-class debate.

There are also substantive constraints. For cases involving racial or gender issues, it is particularly important that various views be represented. Along these lines, some cases have specific legal implications that students might be assigned to explore, such as aspects of tort law.

In general, cases can be planned around a variety of instructional and course objectives, many of which have been noted earlier in this Introduction. These include:

- Indirect socialization through exposure to real-world experiences in case form
- Development of a personal repertoire of responses and behaviors to common but difficult situations that might otherwise be unknown to the student
- Developing skills in separating fact from assumption, and in deducing details from outlines
- Practicing the articulation of objectives and the formulation of strategy in administrative settings involving personal, organizational, and interorganizational relations
- Experience in withholding judgment and resisting the temptation to jump to conclusions before the facts are assessed and diverse views heard
- Improving one's capacity for relating textbook theory to practical settings
- Experience in group problem analysis and resolution
- Improving diagnostic skills and skills at designing effective interventions into administrative settings
- Testing one's personal values and objectives
- Acquiring greater facility at developing and testing the boundaries of behavioral generalizations

- Relating the "big picture" to the small instance
- Learning how to apply traditional concerns in management and the public service, such as responsiveness, responsibility, and representativeness
- Encouraging risk taking in administrative settings
- Becoming personally aware of the existential dilemmas of public management.

The individual instructor may have many other objectives in using these cases in class and many tactics can facilitate the successful accomplishment of instructional and personal objectives through case usage. Instructors can provide students with an outline to use while reading cases and, perhaps, ask students to write each assignment in a standard format. One format, suggested by Professor Ross Clayton of the University of Southern California, has a number of variations in common use. The students are requested to identify or provide the following:

- What are the facts available in the case?
- What are the assumptions made in the case?
- What conclusions do you draw from these facts and assumptions?
- What theories, common prescriptions, or legal doctrines are relevant to this case?
- What experiences have you had that come to mind when reading this case, and what have you learned from these experiences that helps you here?
- What recommendations do you make, for whom, and why?

When employing an analytical paradigm of this sort, the students should focus on the concrete rather than on prescriptive generalities such as "follow the steps of a rational decision" or "invite the participation of all concerned."

In a brief article about "process methods" Professor Harold Fox* of DePaul University offers a number of practical suggestions about using cases. He asserts that "most classes contain some members who read carelessly, and therefore fail to grasp the point or points of a case." He suggests requesting students to prepare a statement of the objectives of a case in order to condense the case into a few carefully chosen words;

---

*Harold W. Fox, "Two Dozen Ways of Handling Cases: Depending on How You Count," *Collegiate News and Views* XXVI: 3 (Spring 1973).

translate the contents of the case into textbook language and terminology; separate fact from opinion (similar to the paradigm preceding); or prepare a diagram relating the central problems of a case and all the collateral factors associated with it.

Many group-involvement techniques can assist the class in getting the most from a case. Fox suggests the "Phillips 66" technique in which the class is divided into groups of six, which then have six minutes to form a position and select a leader to present it. The instructor can also hand a class predetermined solutions for a case and invite justification or criticism. A class can be divided into teams for preparation of written or oral reports. An interesting variation on this common classroom technique, implied by Fox, is for the instructor to recommend different ways of dividing the work among different groups. Then the class can observe the consequences of group structure upon each group's decisions. Role playing in front of the class has been suggested. Several of the cases in this book lend themselves particularly well to this technique, which often involves extending the action beyond the narrative.

The contents can also be altered to gain insight into a case. Fox poses questions like, "What changes in the setting would call for substantial change in the solution?" This alerts case analysts to "sensitivity" questions. Occasionally an instructor may invite managers who have experience dealing with the issues or settings of a case to speak to the class. This can vary classroom pace and add practical insight. Fox also recommends having the class seek analogies to a case situation in current events or in academic writings as a means of "mind stretching."

Fox suggests several techniques to heighten the students' ability to apply insights derived from case analysis. One technique is to ask students to deal with generic situations to which an inventory of probable solutions can be crafted. This technique fosters the development and refinement of principles of action, and the recognition of structural commonalties in managerial situations. One common situation is that of the "new employee on the job," which is presented in "The Making of a Corrections Officer" (Case 43). The students might be assigned the task of developing guidelines for anyone taking on a new supervisory role in a setting fraught with problems.

Another technique for promoting the application of case learning is to have the students conduct class or have the students write cases themselves and share them with the class. If this latter technique is chosen, however, it is important to provide the students with guidelines for writing a case. Among the most important are: (a) make cases decision-oriented rather than just descriptive of a situation *and* include identifiable issue(s); (b) write the case from the perspective of a specific person, even if that person does not appear directly in the case; and (c) provide sufficient information in the case to use as a basis for making a decision or recommendation.

Each case in this volume can be used in several ways. We hope instructors can use the material in this Introduction to encourage creativity in the classroom. We also hope we have made clear the extent to which the cases in this book represent a substantial and flexible pedagogical resource. We welcome constructive advice about the use of the cases, and we hope our suggestions help students and instructors to get the most out of them.

Table A-1. Classification of Cases by Managerial Issues

Legend:
● Major topic of case
✔ Other relevant topics

Case	ADA Issues	Bargaining & Negotiations	Communication	Community/Client Relations	Collaboration	Conflict & Cooperation	Ethical Questions	Leadership Issues	Organizational Change & Culture	Organizational Structure	Personal Dilemmas	Personnel Actions	Policies & Procedures	Sexual Conduct	Social Problems	Staff Relations	Total Quality Management	Training
PART ONE — BARGAINING & NEGOTIATIONS																		
1. A Tiger in the Planning Section											●		✔			✔		
2. ACLU v. Tyler County		●	✔	✔														
3. Budget Cuts		●				✔		✔										
4. Commercial Free Speech?			✔		●								✔					
5. Intransigence and Inertia		●	✔								✔							
6. Middle Management Ignored		●										✔	✔					
7. Who Staffs the Hospital?		●				✔						✔						
PART TWO — ETHICAL & PERSONAL DILEMMAS																		
8. A Zealous City Employee						✔	●						✔					
9. AIDS Patients	✔						●											
10. Ann's Dilemma						✔	●				✔		✔					
11. A Case of Bureaucratic Morality?							●						✔	✔				
12. Anna Lieberman, Deceased				✔		✔					●							
13. One Perspective on Hillsdale Tower			✔								●		✔					
14. The Outsider						✔	●									✔		
15. Thompson's Time Management			✔			✔					●							
PART THREE — ORGANIZATIONAL & LEADERSHIP ISSUES																		
16. Agency Capture?				✔		✔			●									
17. Deliah's In-Basket						✔	✔		●	●								
18. Dilemma in Juvenile Court						✔			●									✔
19. Effective Leadership?								●				✔	✔					
20. Going to the Dogs!			✔			✔		●										
21. Hail to the New Chief						✔		●	✔									
22. Shifting the Costs of Governance		✔								●							✔	

continues

Table A-1. Classification of Cases by Managerial Issues, continued

Legend:
- ● Major topic of case
- ✔ Other relevant topics

	ADA Issues	Bargaining & Negotiations	Communication	Community/Client Relations	Collaboration	Conflict & Cooperation	Ethical Questions	Leadership Issues	Organizational Change & Culture	Organizational Structure	Personal Dilemmas	Personnel Actions	Policies & Procedures	Sexual Conduct	Social Problems	Staff Relations	Total Quality Management	Training
PART FOUR — ORGANIZATIONAL CULTURE & CHANGE																		
23. A License for Quality: TQM at the BMV									✔				✔				●	
24. Doing Hard Time: Reforming the Prison System								✔	●	✔								
25. Environmental Quality				✔					●	✔								
26. Mixed Effects of a Demonstration Project								✔	●						✔			
PART FIVE — PERSONNEL & HUMAN RESOURCE ISSUES																		
27. A Supervisor for Unit II												●				✔		✔
28. Affirmative Action in Hamilton County											✔	●				✔		
29. HIV and Employee Rights	●											✔						✔
30. Performance Evaluation and Organizational Rigidity												●	✔			✔		
31. The Police Captain Dilemma											✔	●				✔		
32. Reasonable Accommodation	●											✔		✔		✔		
33. A Subordinate's Homophobia							✔					●		✔				✔
PART SIX — POLICIES & PROCEDURES																		
34. A Matter of Evaluation								✔	✔		✔		●					
35. Annual Daffodil Festival			✔					✔					●					
36. Metropolitan Emergency Medical Services				✔							✔				●			
37. Of Bounded Cooperation		✔										✔	●					
38. The *Challenger* Shuttle Disaster		✔				●							✔					
39. The Gesture That Went Awry							●					✔	●					

continues

Table A-1.   Classification of Cases by Managerial Issues, continued

	● Major topic of case ✔ Other relevant topics	ADA Issues	Bargaining & Negotiations	Communication	Community/Client Relations	Collaboration	Conflict & Cooperation	Ethical Questions	Leadership Issues	Organizational Change & Culture	Organizational Structure	Personal Dilemmas	Personnel Actions	Policies & Procedures	Sexual Conduct	Social Problems	Staff Relations	Total Quality Management	Training
PART SEVEN																			
SUPERVISORY PROBLEMS																			
40.	An Office Romance						✔								●		✔		
41.	Carl the Ripper												✔		●		✔		
42.	Conflicts on the Human Services Coordination Team		✔				●										✔		
43.	The Making of a Corrections Officer							✔	✔								●		
44.	Distributing County Property Without Consent						✔							●			✔		
45.	Easing Toward Change in Urbania's Finance Department		✔							✔							●		
46.	"Keep a Two-by-Four Behind Your Desk"									✔				✔			●		
47.	"Stop Having Birthdays"						●		✔			✔					●		
48.	One Supervisor's Analysis											✔					✔	●	

PART ONE

Bargaining and Negotiations

		Page
1.	A Tiger in the Planning Section	21
2.	ACLU v. Tyler County	24
3.	Budget Cuts	30
4.	Commercial Free Speech?	32
5.	Intransigence and Inertia	35
6.	Middle Management Ignored	41
7.	Who Staffs the Hospital?	46

1

A Tiger in the Planning Section

Jim Dailey has requested a special meeting with Phil Lucas, Director of the Planning Section in an agency of state government. Today is the day, an unusual day, for it is seldom that Jim deals with Phil Lucas in a direct way. Phil is the boss of Jim's immediate superior, Fred Harkness. Phil is clearly a man of power and high potential who has made his mark at an early age. Moreover, Jim feels it is strong evidence of Phil's respect for him that Jim's request for an appointment was filled so promptly. Jim believes, in short, that Phil is a man like himself and that both men recognize that similarity.

Jim is a self-styled organizational tiger. He has prepared himself well for what he sees as a struggle in which the smartest and most adaptable take home the biggest prizes. He has his MPA from an outstanding school; his fine mind and skills have been honed with a disciplined rigor; and he has a look-at-me skill with a variety of exotic quantitative and data-processing techniques.

Jim has quickly become a key employee in the Planning Section for the agency. In some areas, indeed, he approaches indispensability. This is particularly the case in his contribution to the design and early programming of a complex Management Information System (MIS), now approaching completion.

The tiger model had come to Jim during one of those nonverbal games that his friends like to play at their parties. He usually does not disguise his disinterest in such foolishness, but that night was different, perhaps because of the attractive young woman who was egging him on. The game is a simple one. The party goers pair off, act out behaviors of their favorite animal for a few minutes, and then discuss among themselves their feelings and reactions to the animal-self.

Jim was into the game quickly, and in a rare moment for him, he became an observer, watching himself go out of control. Jim had caught the fascinated eye of his partner with his acting before he realized what animal he was playing. He was *el tigre*, the big cat: lean, competent, and swift, circling till his need and the proper opportunity triggered a quick leap at the jugular of some available target. Jim let that picture run through his mind. He liked the fantasy, even the part where his bachelor apartment becomes the cave to which he returns to savor his conquests or to lick his wounds and plan for retribution. The analogy breaks down only when it comes to motivation. Hunger and perhaps fear move the big cat, and they come but occasionally; but whatever moves Jim is almost always there, goading him even when he knows he should remain careful and controlled, which is most of the time.

The story about Jim-as-tiger got back to work, and even then he relishes the image. "Hey, tiger!" is often heard around the office, and not always aloud or in a friendly tone of voice. Jim is aware of some of the unflattering and private references to "the tiger," but he discounts them. Mostly, he reasons, the whispers come from the losers who can neither help him nor hurt him. The losers can have their little joke: He is after bigger game.

Today, in meeting with Phil, Jim is surely the tiger. He has been careful since he joined the Planning Section, although he has been revealing increasingly more of his plan to selected colleagues. They do not encourage him, but, more important to Jim, they do not warn him to stop. Jim learns two lessons from this: He is a man others reckon with carefully, and his central argument is widely credible.

Today is the day to be really bold. Jim's approach to Phil is direct:

"Phil, you know me.

"I have done a good job for you and the Planning Section. I appreciate the early opportunity, but I am doing far more than anyone expected of me.

"Despite this feeling of accomplishment, life in the section is becoming intolerable for me. Fred Harkness can't cut the work; that's increasingly clear. And I shouldn't carry his load and mine, too, unless I get the recognition soon. And I won't do double duty in silence any longer.

"You know my generation, Phil. We tell it like it is. And if we get bombed for that, we pack it up. A professional cannot do it any other way.

"I hope *I* can tell it like it is."

∾o∾
INSTRUCTIONS AND QUESTIONS

You are Phil Lucas. How do you respond to Dailey? Your response should be based on at least four items of information:

1. Fred Harkness is a good personal friend of yours and a loyal agency employee. He is 62 and clearly no match for Dailey in his knowledge of systems analysis and data processing.

2. Jim Dailey's usefulness to the agency is at an immediate peak right now. In six to nine months, when the MIS system is designed and largely in place, you are convinced that Harkness can handle the job as well as, and probably better than, Dailey. Harkness has that touch with people, you believe.

3. You are not certain, but it seems unlikely that Planning will have another job soon on which Dailey's skills and knowledge will be critical.

4. You feel Dailey has real potential for advancement and would like to retain him in anticipation of cashing in on this potential. But you are convinced that, unless his attitude changes, Dailey will be more trouble than he is worth.

2

ACLU v. Tyler County

12TH CIRCUIT COURT OF APPEALS
UNITED STATES OF AMERICA

November

Greetings:

Pursuant to recent rulings by this Court, and in agreement with the accord between parties to *American Civil Liberties Union v. Tyler County*, we hereby determine that the Tyler County office of the state Department of Human Services (DHS) must, in all good faith and expeditious action, (1) negotiate an equitable settlement with appropriate parties and (2) make plans and carry out a strategy to deliver the following services:

1. Convenient and prompt issuance of federally sponsored food stamps
2. Regular and timely distribution of surplus food products
3. Fair treatment to all residents concerning government-subsidized housing
4. Access to job training and employment services
5. Provision of support furnishings such as excess clothes, furniture, foodstuffs
6. Availability of family and individual counseling
7. Access to transportation services in both urban and rural areas
8. Inexpensive and comprehensive health services to include both primary and secondary medical care and health prevention (wellness) programs

Further, we instruct (1) the administrator of the Tyler County DHS office to report quarterly to his/her superiors at the state DHS office concerning progress in these actions and (2) the state administrator to inform this Court of said progress on an annual basis.

Signed this ___1st___ day of _____November_____.

_____

Bridget Ryan, Presiding Judge

PEOPLE HELPING PEOPLE
Department of Human Services
Tyler County

Memo to:	All Department Heads
From:	Jose Espinosa
Subject:	Determination Letter from U.S. 12th Circuit Court of Appeals
Date:	November

By now you have all had a chance to read the letter from the Court, directing us to work with service providers in our area to guarantee social services to eligible recipients in this county. I have just spoken by phone with state DHS director Bill Knight, who has emphasized the importance of our abiding by the court's determination and the settlement in the case referred to in the Court's letter. I certainly second his concern and direct you to work together with welfare rights groups, unions, citizens and elected officials, and relevant nonprofits in the county to make this happen.

Specifically, I am assigning Delphinia Wharton, Director of Case Management, to lead this effort. She will be in touch with each one of you about actions to be taken.

Note to Delphinia: Thanks for your willingness to take on this job. I am relieving you of all internal responsibilities so that you can concentrate on this project. — Jose

UNITED WAY OF TYLER COUNTY

Memo to: Stephen Nix, Planning Director
From: Elizabeth Walker, Director and CEO
Subject: Collaboration with DHS
Date: November

Steve, I just got off the phone with Delphinia Wharton over at DHS. I know you've worked with her on other projects. She is in a panic. She has just been handed a huge assignment by Mr. Espinosa—something about carrying out court orders that came out of the ACLU case of last year. Why don't you give her a call and see how we can help? You may want to talk with some of our agency directors, especially Red Cross, Food Bank, Family and Children Services, and Meals on Wheels, to get their input and cooperation. This is going to be a big one and we'll need to crank up our network of service providers all across the county.

AMERICAN RED CROSS
Tyler County

Memo to: Varena Stalker, Director
             Division of Health and Human Services
From: Elliott Levy, Chapter Manager
Subject: Comprehensive Services Project in Tyler County
Date: November

Vee, Steve Nix just called to tell me about the DHS project of pulling together social service agencies across the county to satisfy the court ruling in *ACLU v. Tyler County*. Sounds like a big project that will need to include every agency in any way connected with health and human services. Also, he said Delphinia Wharton over at DHS was asked to direct the project. She's fairly new to the county so she'll need some help. Have any ideas?

From the Desk of Varena Stalker...

Elliott: Here's what I'd do.

1. Since Delphinia is relatively new to Tyler County, she should call David Flint over at Tyler Tech (555-9972) to get his help in pulling

together this group of agencies. I've worked with him a lot and he's good. He has done a lot of this kind of collaboration and could facilitate the work.

2. She should get in touch with Jenny Gauld at the Nonprofit Center (555-8146), who has done some negotiating work. That's not her main job, but she is sharp and a quick learner. She may be able to help with the clients and other recipient groups.

3. Has anyone called the county manager? He's effective, even though he's pretty busy keeping the county commissioners out of trouble. Local government ought to be brought in, for both their resources and their political clout with state agencies.

4. Don't let Delphinia go off half-cocked. This will take some planning.

5. And, finally (between you and me), watch out for the folks over at United Way. They'll try to take over the whole show if you let them.

TYLER COUNTY COMMISSION
Keeping Tyler County Green for Its Citizens
Office of the Manager

November

Ms. Delphinia Wharton, Director
Division of Case Management
Tyler County Department of Human Services

Dear Ms. Wharton:

I have not had the pleasure of meeting you yet, but want to welcome you to Tyler County. We here in the courthouse are eager to help you in any way possible.

To that end, I understand that you have been entrusted with the task of carrying out the directives of the 12th Circuit Court of Appeals concerning the ACLU social services case of last year. We are sympathetic with the enormity of that task and pledge our resources if we can be of service.

Perhaps you would want to hold your meetings here in the courthouse. We could provide you with refreshments and a part-time secretary if that would help.

Please call me and tell me how I can assist you. Prompt resolution of this case is in all of our interests.

Sincerely,

Bill Donald
County Manager

Phone message
To: Dr. Flint   Date: 11/19   Time: 1:15 P.M.
Ms. Delphinia Wharton at DHS telephoned (555-3211). She wants to talk to you about your helping on a collaborative effort.
DWS

Phone message
To: Ms. Gauld   Date: 11/19   Time: 1:30 P.M.
Ms. Delphinia Wharton of DHS (555-3211) called. Please call ASAP. She is interested in talking to you about some negotiating and mediation.
Judy

(Confidential memo for file)   David Flint
11/19
Returned call from a Delphinia Wharton. We talked in detail about my helping her on collaborative effort related to ACLU decision from Court of Appeals. She said she was calling Jenny Gauld and wanted my advice. I told her Jenny is first-rate. D. will get back to me.

11/20
Talked with Jenny today. We agreed to help Delphinia Wharton with two-pronged strategy to negotiate a "treaty" with plaintiffs and clients and to try to collaborate with other stakeholders who will be asked to help deliver services and provide information and referral. Jenny excited about project, but in time crunch as I am. I offered my assistant as backup.

11/22
Met with Jenny and Delphinia today. D. is sharp but inexperienced. She'll do fine, but will need our assistance and advice. Agreed that Jenny would lead negotiation and I would help put together public-private-nonprofit partnership. We will propose strategy for both and we'll fine-

tune. On tight timeline so will ask my assistant to turn in proposal by 12/6.

❦

INSTRUCTIONS AND QUESTIONS

You are the assistant to David Flint. He asks you to help him and Ms. Gauld design a strategy to assist Delphinia Wharton. Additionally, he asks you to analyze the process in a supporting paper.

Your response should be in two parts:

1. Write a detailed memo to Flint and Gauld outlining a plan to assist Wharton accomplish the charge from the Court. Since Wharton has never led a project of this magnitude and is eager to receive advice and assistance, you should be thorough in your proposal,

2. Analyze and draft the strategy you have proposed as it relates to collaboration.

3

Budget Cuts

You work for a small governmental agency known as the Policy Analysis Support Agency (PASA). PASA is divided into five small divisions, each doing policy and data research for all the agencies in state government. A new directive has just come down from the Governor through your Director, Ms. Beecher. The Governor has asked all agencies to project what they would cut if they were to have to reduce their budgets by 10 percent next year. As usual, Ms. Beecher simply passes that request along to each of her division directors. The total PASA budget for next year is $4.1 million.

Division A is the largest division. DIV A, as it is known, does in-depth policy analysis for the two biggest departments in the state, the Health department and the Human Services department. With a budget of just over $1.4 million and an additional $500,000 in grant funds uncontrolled by state funding, DIV A employs 25 full-time policy researchers and related staff on "state monies," and another 10 full-time and 20 part-time on grant funds.

DIV A's annual budget is 35 percent in salaries; 20 percent in hardware; 10 percent travel and professional development; 10 percent office supplies; 25 percent miscellaneous.

Division B is a moderate-size division; it works heavily with the expanding economic development agencies in state government. There have been strong suggestions that a new statewide Department of Commerce is in the works and this division could be transferred to them. DIV B's budget has grown by 15 to 20 percent a year for the last five years, while most of the rest of PASA's budget has remained stable. DIV B has 20 employees on state funds and another 8 on grant funds from the State University's Research Division on Economic Development.

DIV B's budget is $1,250,000: 50 percent salaries; 25 percent hardware; 10 percent travel; 5 percent office supplies; 10 percent miscellaneous.

Division C works with the traditional administrative functions in the older state agencies. Its budget has been shrinking by 10 percent a year, and very few agencies call on DIV C to do their policy work today. Salaried employees number 15, with many years of service, and most have "topped out" in their classified positions in salary. DIV C has no grant or outside monies.

DIV C's budget is $500,000: 75 percent salaries; 15 percent hardware; 5 percent office supplies; 5 percent miscellaneous.

Division D is the smallest division and works with small licensing boards who have little research and policy analysis staff themselves. Its budget has been stable for years, with little dissatisfaction or concern with DIV D's past, present, or future. There are 10 employees; 6 of them are policy analysts.

DIV D's budget is $350,000: 60 percent salaries; 20 percent hardware; 5 percent travel; 5 percent office supplies; 10 percent miscellaneous.

Division E is the "support" division to PASA. This group runs the personnel and finances for PASA and also staffs the data and computer programmers for all of the division's work. DIV E has grown, especially since it gets $20,000 a year in funds from DIV A's and DIV B's grants.

DIV E's budget is $500,000: 40 percent salaries; 40 percent hardware; 5 percent travel; 5 percent office supplies; 10 percent miscellaneous.

᭜ఄ᭜

INSTRUCTIONS AND QUESTIONS

Your job is to propose in what areas the cuts should be defined within a particular PASA division. (Remember, this does NOT mean that the cuts will have to come, only that the Director and Governor want to be prepared for such a decision with good data.)

Define how to come up with the cuts for each division separately. Also, remember the Director's tendency to treat all equally.

4

Commercial Free Speech?

Since Lady Bird Johnson initiated her "Beautify America" campaign in the mid 1960s, a classic confrontation has evolved between business, various special-interest groups, planning commissions, and local governments. The issue of outdoor billboards as a form of "commercial free speech" has caused battle lines to be drawn between the advertising industry, various segments of the community, and local governments.

Many cities have experienced commercial strip growth that follows primary and secondary arterial highway routes. This commercial development also generates a proliferation of billboards, which many environmental advocates refer to as a "blight to the landscape." Many businesses, however, find this particular method of advertising both affordable and effective. The advertising industry, in particular, says that billboards are highly profitable, in part because billboard rentals are not generally subject to a sales tax. All of the billboards have been systematically "permitted" by local and state zoning authorities, according to the area's comprehensive planning blueprint.

Robert Kershaw is a 31-year-old native of Muskogee, Oklahoma, who started his own sign rental business on a part-time basis after securing a small bank loan. A few years later he was able to incorporate his advertising company and operate his business on a full-time basis. At its peak, the Kershaw Advertising Company (KAC) was the largest outdoor advertising company operating exclusively in northeastern Oklahoma, maintaining over 250 portable and permanent sign rentals.

In 1986, with the strong urging of one city council member, the Muskogee City Planning Commission decided to update the existing city codes regulating outdoor billboards and other commercial signs. Some commission members were advocating a total ban on all temporary billboards, the kind of rental units owned by KAC.

A public hearing for citizen input on the matter was held by the Planning Commission. Unfortunately, the discussion of the proposed new sign ordinance was scheduled last on the agenda, after many business people had already gone home. The attorney retained by Mr. Kershaw to represent KAC argued that it was against the U.S. Constitution for a city to impose a total ban on outdoor advertising signs, including temporary billboards. The attorney also stated that federal courts had already ruled that such ordinances violate commercial free speech guaranteed by the Constitution.

The city attorney objected, stating that the majority of local residents thought the signs should be banned for safety and aesthetic reasons. Here in Muskogee, she reported, public safety is the primary concern. Because a driver's vision might be blocked or distracted by an improperly located sign, somebody, probably a child, will step into the street and be seriously injured or killed, she continued. The sign company and the merchant who rented the sign will deny responsibility, and when the smoke clears from the inevitable lawsuit, the city will be held responsible for a sign ordinance that was passed in an attempt to make everybody happy.

The debate and public hearings dragged the affair out for about two years. Ultimately, the Planning Commission decided not to recommend anything to the City Council. City officials continued to argue that they had a legitimate, legal reason for restricting the signs. "It will improve the looks of the city," they said. "And, more importantly, perhaps, prevent traffic hazards caused by distracted motorists." KAC's attorney argued that less restrictive ways were available to prevent traffic hazards.

Opponents of sign reform became very vocal over the next few months, some even calling for the resignation of specific council members and the Fire Chief. They also alerted local merchants to the issue by distributing flyers such as this one:

MERCHANT BEWARE!

The City Council will soon vote on a new sign ordinance that will prohibit or severely restrict your constitutional rights to use many types of signs that advertise your business.

City councilmen have stated that they have not heard from the business community and that you apparently don't care!!

Protect your rights by calling your councilmen and letting them know that you are opposed to any ordinance that places a time limit on the use of portable and ground signs. The Federal Courts have stated that such an attempt would violate the First Amendment of the U.S. Constitution.

Stand up for your rights!! Let the city officials know the will of the people!! Your right to advertise on your own property is not only important to the success of your business, but it's critical to the economic health of our city.

THE AFTERMATH

The City Council of Muskogee finally voted, in 1987, to pass the ordinance but the damage was done. The City Attorney and Robert Kershaw were the only ones remaining who had meaningful input on the drafting of the ordinance, trying to write a new sign ordinance that all parties could live with.

After passage of the new ordinance, the city abandoned all enforcement activity. Local politicians continued to erect permanent signs, and portables were indiscriminately placed around town as if nothing had happened. New competition and new signs flourished in the limited geographic market. In Muskogee, it was obvious that many small, and some not-so-small, businesses found mini-billboards to their liking. Even the City of Muskogee's Parks and Recreation Department rented signs from KAC. The Chamber of Commerce leased four units for the annual Azalea Festival, Muskogee's number-one tourist attraction.

∽o∾

INSTRUCTIONS AND QUESTIONS

1. What are the major public policy considerations that the City Council should analyze prior to adopting a new comprehensive sign ordinance? What additional information do they need?
2. What political considerations will affect the City Council's decision?
3. What, if anything, can Robert Kershaw do to "sell" his proposal to the City Council members?
4. Could this controversy have been resolved before it expanded to a debate on the First Amendment?
5. Who is representing the "public interest" in this case?

5

Intransigence and Inertia

John Hicks is a Senior Administrative Assistant to the Director of the County Public Health Division. Hicks is responsible for the nonmedical administrative activities of more than 200 people (40 of whom are clerical staff) and for a budget of $5.6 million. The clerks staff 18 offices in locations up to 35 miles apart. Coordination of vacation and other extended-leave periods represents his most direct intervention with the clerks' activities. Hicks approves leave requests and provides backup coverage, when necessary.

Clerical staff are represented by a local union affiliated with the AFL-CIO, which recently won a jurisdictional dispute to represent the clerical employees. The union negotiated a clause into the Memorandum of Understanding (MOU) providing a higher rate of pay for staff temporarily assigned to a higher level or classification (Work Out of Classification, or WOC). Exhibit 5-1 provides the text of this clause.

Coincidental with these negotiations, the department head's secretary requested a reclassification of her position to a higher level. The personnel department studied her job and refused to reclassify it. This action was not accepted graciously. The secretary became very active in union business, recruiting new members and insisting on strict administration of the MOU.

Shortly after execution of the Memorandum, a Typist Clerk II (TC-2) position became vacant due to a retirement. This vacancy did not fall within the definition of a temporary vacancy. Hicks assigned a Typist Clerk I (TC-1) to cover the vacant desk—to handle only routine typing, filing, and telephone-reception activities, all of which are expected of a TC-1. The TC-1 requested WOC pay for the assignment. After consultation with the personnel department, Hicks refused the request for two reasons.

1. A temporary vacancy does not exist.
2. The assigned activities are within those expected of a TC-1.

The decision and rationale were not accepted. Within a couple of days, via a highly efficient grapevine, the department head's secretary got wind of the situation. The situation provided her a welcome opportunity to nettle the personnel department, and a grievance was initiated against Hicks. The personnel department's labor-relations officer, after listening to the union position and having one brief telephone consultation with Hicks, reversed his earlier decision and awarded WOC pay to the TC-1.

A year later, the county experienced a financial crisis resulting in multiple layoffs and involuntary demotions. One involuntary demotion affected a clerk—Ella Fitzpatrick—who only two months before had been promoted by reclassification. The reclassification action occurred glacially; it took over two years to obtain approval, only to have an additional four months elapse before official enactment. Two months after enactment, due to the elimination of a position in another division, the newly promoted individual was "bumped," with only two options: accept a layoff or take a demotion. Just prior to the effective date of the demotion, Hicks's own secretary resigned. After a brief interview with Fitzpatrick, Hicks offered her the position in his office. A demotion was still involved, but not back to the position she occupied prior to the reclassification.

Among her other duties, Fitzpatrick provided primary coverage for vacations or other extended-leave periods. Within a year of her assumption of the new position, Hicks verbally assigned her to cover his boss's secretary's position—at a higher-level. The timing of covering the boss's office was less than convenient—the Christmas/New Year's holiday period and also the time when the following year's budget is being prepared. Fitzpatrick was required to serve as the division director's secretary for 17 days. Ten days into this assignment, she asked Hicks whether she was eligible for WOC pay for the last seven days of the assignment. Hicks believed she was eligible but realized that requests for WOC pay require approval by the personnel director. Since there had been numerous instances of past retroactive approvals of such requests, and considering the labor-relations officer's award to the TC-1 two years earlier, Hicks did not anticipate significant obstacles. He advised Fitzpatrick that he would review the MOU and figure out how to handle a tardy request. However, due to the press of budget work, Hicks did not get around to searching for a solution for two days.

Unaware that a retroactive WOC request was in the works, the labor-relations officer issued a memorandum to "department heads" concerning administration of the WOC clause of the contract. Perhaps because he was a "senior administrative assistant" and not a "department head," Hicks did not receive a copy of the memo. It established two criteria for approval of WOC requests: the assignment must be made in writing and the request must be approved *in advance* by the personnel director. The former criterion was stipulated in the MOU, but the latter was not.

Unaware, Hicks called the personnel director for advice on how to proceed in Fitzpatrick's case and ran into a stone wall. In spite of past practices, the failure to disseminate WOC procedures adequately, and the fact that the assignment occurred prior to issuance of the new WOC procedures, the personnel director stated that he would reject a retroactive request. Hicks advised him of the militancy of union members in the department and also warned that a formal grievance could result.

Hicks advised Fitzpatrick, now back at her own desk, of the personnel director's position. Hicks still hoped that by consulting other top administrators he could construct a case for approval. Hicks asked Fitzpatrick to refrain from involving the union until there was a response to his written request.

Hicks sent a memorandum through his boss to the personnel director, admitting to two counts of personal administrative negligence in connection with Fitzpatrick's WOC assignment—his failure to order the assignment in written form and his failure to get advance approval from the personnel director. Hicks suggested that a mechanism ought to exist whereby administrative errors can be corrected, short of resorting to a formal grievance.

A couple of weeks passed without reply. Rather than responding directly to Hicks, the personnel director consulted with the department head, convincing him that the request should be refused. The department head refused the request in writing, directing his response to Hicks's boss with copies to Hicks and Fitzpatrick.

Hicks, believing that his secretary should not be the scapegoat in this situation, advised Fitzpatrick to initiate a formal grievance and to request union assistance.

Fitzpatrick called the union, advising the business agent of the situation. The agent requested copies of Hicks's and the department head's memos. The agent also advised Fitzpatrick to obtain the assistance of a former shop steward to prepare the grievance.

Upon reviewing the correspondence, union officials felt they had a solid case. They began by writing the county's labor-relations officer, summarizing the grievance and providing documentation of the situation. They requested a response within the time limits established in the MOU grievance procedure.

The labor relations officer's responsibility involved reviewing the grievance to determine whether any violations of the Memorandum had occurred, advising the county manager that a grievance had been filed, and rendering the county's response to the grievance. After consulting with the personnel director, the labor-relations officer responded that the county had not violated the MOU. He claimed that lack of written assignment and prior approval constituted grounds for denying the grievance.

The union did not agree and appealed to the county manager—the next step in the grievance process. One of the county manager's staff was assigned to handle the grievance. After consulting with the personnel director, the labor-relations officer, and the union and not being able to resolve the grievance, the issue was scheduled for an Adjustment Board hearing.

The Adjustment Board consists of three people appointed by management and three people appointed by the union. The board serves a quasi-judicial role, adjudicating grievances not resolved at lower levels.

The Adjustment Board is the step in the grievance process immediately preceding rights arbitration.

The amount of pay potentially owed to Fitzpatrick was approximately $235.00.

Exhibit 5-1.   Relevant Language in the Memorandum of
Understanding

Section 27. Change of Assigned Duties
No employee shall be required regularly to perform duties of a
position outside of the classification to which he/she has been appointed. However, employees may be temporarily assigned duties
outside their classification. In addition, under the conditions described in the Rules of the Civil Service Commission, a department head may temporarily assign to employees whatever duties
are necessary to meet the requirements of an emergency situation.

Section 28. Pay for Work Out of Classification

When an employee has been assigned in writing by the department head or designated representative to perform the work of a permanent position having a different classification and being paid at a higher rate, and if he/she has worked in such classification for more than ten (10) consecutive workdays, he/she shall be entitled to payment for the higher classification, as prescribed for *Promotions* in Section 5.5 of this Memorandum of Understanding, starting on the eleventh (11th) workday and continuing during the period of temporary assignment, under the following conditions:

(1) The assignment is caused by the temporary absence of the incumbent;

(2) The employee performs the duties regularly performed by the temporarily absent incumbent, and these duties are clearly not included in the job description of his/her regular classification; and

(3) The temporary assignment to work out of classification is approved by the Personnel Director, a copy of the approval form to be given to the employee.

Section 29. Dismissal, Suspension, or Demotion for Cause

The appointing authority may dismiss, suspend for not more than thirty (30) days, or demote any employee in the classified service provided the rules and regulations of the Civil Service Commission are followed. If he/she does not appeal such action to the Civil Service Commission within fourteen (14) days after receipt of such charges, as provided in Section 13, Article XIV of the Charter, a permanent employee shall have the right to appeal such action in accordance with the provisions of Section 30.2.... (4) A permanent classified employee may be dismissed, suspended, or demoted for cause only.

Section 30. Grievances

30.1 A grievance is any dispute which involves the interpretation of application of any provision of this Memorandum of Understanding excluding, however, those provisions of this Memorandum of Understanding which specifically provide that the decision of any county official shall be final, the interpretation or application of those provisions not being subject to the grievance procedure.

30.2 Grievances shall be processed in the following manner:

(1) Any employee who believes that he/she has a grievance may discuss his/her complaint with such management official in the department in which he/she works as the department head may designate. If the issue is not resolved within the department, or if the employee elects to submit his/her grievance directly to the union recognized as the representative of his/her classification, the procedures hereinafter specified may be invoked....

∽o∽
INSTRUCTIONS AND QUESTIONS

1. What do you think the Adjustment Board's decision ought to be?
2. At what stage(s) could or should this grievance have been settled? What precluded its settlement?
3. Should the county manager have intervened earlier?
4. How long do you juggle ethics and organizational justice? Does price tag affect the decision and how long it takes to make it?
5. You are the county manager. Do you fire Hicks for starting this whole mess?
6. You are Hicks. What does this apparently petty situation mean for you and your career?

6

Middle Management Ignored*

In 1990, officers of the Gardner City Police Department became affiliated with the American Federation of State, County, and Municipal Employees (AFSCME). At this time, the middle-management ranks of the Gardner City Police Department, especially sergeants, lieutenants, and captains, decided not to be represented by the union.

At the beginning, the benefits AFSCME gained through the collective-bargaining process were small and automatically given to middle management. AFSCME has now been in operation for six years and during the last two years has won some very good fringe benefits and wage increases for its members.

In 1993, AFSCME invited middle management to join the union. The middle-management echelon of the police department was the only group in Gardner City not affiliated. The fire department had been totally organized since the inception of the firemen's union. The police middle management met and discussed the offer to join AFSCME. They decided not to join since it would be detrimental to the mission of the officers. They also felt that their affiliation with a union would cast a shadow of doubt as to where their loyalty rested. This decision on the part of middle management left them without any representation in regard to benefits and wages.

Up until this time, the city manager, through the city council, had immediately passed on all union gains to middle management without a request from them. One of the issues included in the 1990 contract

*This case was prepared by Richard M. Ayres, FBI Academy, and Thomas L. Wheelen, McIntire School of Commerce.

was a 10-cent night-shift differential. This benefit, however, was not passed on to middle management.

In the 1993 negotiations, more new benefits were gained for union members. Middle management, once again, did not receive any of these new benefits. As a result of this action, middle management decided it was time to bring these inequities to the attention of the City Manager. A formal letter (Exhibit 6-1), was drafted and sent to the City Manager. The City Manager then wrote a reply (Exhibit 6-2) to their letter, responding to their expressed inequities.

Exhibit 6-1.   Letter to City Manager of Gardner City

February 14, 1993

Dear Sir:

We, the members of the supervisory and management echelon of the Gardner City Police Department, would like to take this opportunity, with all due respect, to voice our collective opinion regarding several inequities that we believe may develop from the ranks and which are not included in the bargaining unit.

We consider our echelon—supervision and management—as an extension or arm of the city manager and the chief of police, and as such our loyalty must and does in fact remain with these administrators. We have vividly demonstrated this loyalty in the past by voting against our inclusion in the bargaining unit representing the operational echelon of the department.

Recently, in what appeared to be a job action by members of the department bargaining unit, the responsibility for providing police protection fell on the shoulders of supervisory personnel, whose loyalty was demonstrated by reporting for duty and performing all required services for the citizens of Gardner City. We feel that in order to prevent a conflict of interests and to perpetuate the strong loyalty to the administration, we cannot and should not become affiliated with a bargaining unit. No individual can serve two masters and be equally loyal to each.

However, self-preservation and self-esteem are the two most intense behavioral drives possessed by humans, and to these ends we have composed this communication.

First and of long-standing concern to our numbers is the inequity which exists between bargaining-unit members and our ranks with respect to the night-shift differential. The night-shift differential had been in existence for several years and was not initially offered to nonunion employees nor has it ever been discussed with our members. Currently, only eight supervisors would be concerned with this pay differential, but it is an inequity to the supervisory ranks of the department.

The next area of concern to nonunion personnel is the apparent fact that the bargaining unit has obtained an additional uniform allowance. No additional allowances were forthcoming to supervisors, which was both embarrassing and thought-provoking. Embarrassing since it was apparent on that payday when two checks were received by union employees and none by supervisors that "you guys don't rate," a somewhat grating statement heard by most supervisors upon reporting for pay. Thought-provoking in that if initially we were not included in the night-shift differential and subsequently not included in the allocation of funds for additional uniform allowance, it is apparent that the future is not getting brighter for supervisors who are loyal nonunion members.

These inequities should not have accrued at the outset. To allow the initial oversight to carry over from year to year and to overlook the appropriation of funds to guarantee those additional benefits to supervisors is most detrimental to the morale of the supervisory echelon.

We respectfully request that the nonunion supervisors of the police department be placed on parity with other city employees and that this be standard for each subsequent contractual agreement. This would eliminate the annual apprehension and the requirement that we must communicate inequities on a yearly basis.

We request that these aforementioned conditions be considered in the light of fairness, equality, and an opportunity to provide a prideful environment for supervisors who are not union-affiliated.

Respectfully,

Supervisors of the Gardner City Police Department

Exhibit 6-2.   Letter to Chief of Police of Gardner City

February 27, 1993

Dear Chief:

This is in reply to the letter dated February 14, 1993, signed by all sergeants, lieutenants, and captains, in which they set forth certain alleged inequities in the benefits offered to nonunion personnel.

I would point out that, with the exception of the Chief and Assistant Chief, all other supervisors receive overtime pay at the rate of one and one-half times regular wages. This benefit is not extended to any other supervisor in Gardner.

In addition, I must remind you that last year the classifications for Chief and Assistant Chief were upgraded in order to compensate for the lack of time-and-one-half provisions in these two positions.

In order for me to secure money to implement the request contained in their letter, it will be necessary for me to request an additional appropriation. If you will provide me with the cost figures to cover the numerous requests made, I will present them to the city council.

Very truly yours,

City Manager

∽○∾
INSTRUCTIONS AND QUESTIONS

The City Manager's request for cost figures, he realizes, will buy only a little time. And he feels the need for a thorough review.

So he puts his administrative intern—you—on the project of developing materials to rethink all of the issues. For starters, the City Manager gives you six questions to research and to think about. He wants a study memo from you in a week, although you will still have to carry on your normal duties.

1. What factors presented in this case would cause middle management to unionize?

2. What problems can you foresee in permitting supervisory personnel to be members of a police officer's union.
   a. Would the police officers be reluctant to file grievances against their supervisors?
   b. Would supervisors be reluctant to take appropriate and often needed disciplinary action against subordinates?
   c. Would the supervisors be reluctant to side with management during a job action?
3. Should the city council automatically pass on to middle management benefits that police officers gained through contract negotiations?
4. What is middle management's real source of dissatisfaction as depicted in this case? Recognition? Full appreciation of work done? Financial rewards?
5. What would be middle management's expected response to the City Manager's letter?
6. How should this labor-relations crisis be prevented in the future?

7

Who Staffs the Hospital?

Bentley Memorial is a 250-bed, private hospital and a member of Associated Hospitals, a collective-bargaining association acting on behalf of all member hospitals. The Association has been bargaining with the union representing registered nurses (RNs) concerning contract issues. One important issue has not been resolved: whether management has the right to assign general-duty nurses to special care units such as the Intensive Care Unit (ICU) or the Cardiac Care Unit (CCU). Management has stated that such an assignment would be made only when staffing shortages arise in these units and when there is no other alternative. This utilization of general-duty nurses in a specialty area would take place only when no specially trained staff members are available, and appropriate precautions would be taken to ensure that patient care is safeguarded and adequate supervision and support for the staff is maintained. To date, the practice has been uniform among member hospitals, and they remain united as to the necessity of such a practice.

The union representing the RNs disagrees strongly with the hospital's position. Union officials contend that it is unfair to general-duty nurses to require them to work in a specialized unit for which they have neither training nor experience, and that such a staffing practice is unsafe and unfair to the patients.

Although this issue has been discussed during previous bargaining sessions between management and the union, no settlement has been reached. There are indications that the union will attempt to force a resolution in its favor in upcoming contract negotiations.

It is a Saturday afternoon about three months before the contract negotiations are scheduled to begin. Susan James, Nursing Supervisor for the evening shift and the sole administrative officer on duty, arrives at Bentley Memorial to begin work on the evening shift. After receiving the intershift report from Brad Buford, the day-shift supervisor, Susan discusses with Brad a staffing problem that has arisen in ICU. Three members of the ICU nursing staff have called in sick during the day shift, and there are no replacements available. None of the day staff is willing to work overtime, and both supervisors have tried unsuccessfully to obtain temporary personnel through outside agencies that the hospital has used in the past. They decide to review the RNs who are on duty for the evening shift to determine who they can place in ICU.

After reviewing the staff roster, Susan and Brad narrow the choice down to either Sarah Williams or Helen Beck. Sarah Williams has had several years of ICU experience, but she was recently transferred to general floor duty. This transfer was made by the Director of Nursing as a result of several documented instances of poor judgment in critical-care situations and of problems involving her technical competence for ICU duty. Because of this transfer, Sarah has become extremely hostile toward the nursing supervisors. As a result of these factors, Brad and Susan decide not to send Sarah to ICU.

Helen Beck is an experienced general-duty nurse who has been working at Bentley for three years. She has worked in ICU many times in the past and has not voiced many objections. Moreover, Helen has seemed to be somewhat bored with her job recently. For the past few months she has been less enthusiastic about her work and she has been fulfilling only the minimum requirements in both quality and quantity on the job, in contrast to the excellent work she had done previously. She has also become increasingly friendly with union representatives and with several RNs who have demonstrated hostile attitudes toward hospital administration and the nursing department. However, Susan still believes that Helen is the best replacement available for ICU that evening.

Susan evaluates the condition of each patient in the ICU, and assigns Helen to care for two patients who are recovering well from surgery and who will require only the type of nursing care that Helen normally administers as a general-duty nurse. Susan also assigns additional support staff to the ICU and informs the nurse in charge of ICU that evening of her decision.

Helen arrives on her regularly scheduled unit and sees the message that she is to work in ICU. She calls the nursing office and speaks with Susan. Helen is not qualified to work in ICU and tells Susan that she does not want to go there. Susan tells Helen that she must go because there is a staffing shortage this evening. Susan tells Helen about the patients she will be caring for and assures her that she will not be required to do anything beyond the scope of her training and experience.

Helen eventually agrees to go to ICU, but states that she will file a union grievance. Susan replies, in a somewhat angry tone, that Helen is free to file a grievance if she wishes.

A few minutes later Helen calls Susan again. The conversation follows:

HELEN: I have decided not to work in ICU. I am not qualified, and the union says that nurses have the right to refuse to work in areas for which they are not qualified. I would be jeopardizing my license if I went. I am standing up for the rights of nurses.

SUSAN (becoming angrier): Are you refusing your assignment, Helen? Refusing an assignment is insubordination, you know.

HELEN: I don't care. I am standing up for the rights of nurses.

SUSAN: Helen, you are qualified to care for the patients you will be assigned to. I have reviewed the assignment myself.

HELEN: Nurses must decide for themselves whether they are qualified, not management.

SUSAN: Refusing an assignment is insubordination, and you'll be suspended for this, Helen.

HELEN: I don't care.

SUSAN: All right, Helen. If you won't go where I've assigned you, you'll have to leave the hospital and not return to work until you can talk to the Director of Nursing on Monday.

The conversation ends.

At this point, Susan calls Donna Hanes, the Director of Nursing, at home and tells her that she's just suspended Helen Beck for insubordination. Donna is concerned about the many possible implications of the action at this particular time and calls the hospital attorney for advice. In the meantime, Susan calls some of the nursing staff who had previously been asked to work overtime and tells them that help is badly needed in ICU. One of the nurses agrees to return for the evening shift.

Susan then begins her routine rounds throughout the hospital. She sees Catherine Tanney on one of the units. Catherine is an older nurse involved in union activities and is extremely hostile toward hospital administration. Catherine tells Susan that she had listened in on the phone conversations between Helen and Susan and that she agrees with Helen's position. Susan tells Catherine in a sharp tone of voice that listening in on phone conversations is illegal and that she is never to do that again at Bentley.

Susan continues on her rounds and arrives at the unit where Helen usually works. She has assumed that Helen has left the hospital after their last conversation but finds her still on the unit answering phones and doing secretarial work for the staff. Susan tells Helen that she has been suspended and must leave the hospital, but Helen says that she will not go and that she wants to stay and work on her regular unit.

The hospital attorney calls Susan to see how things are going. Susan reports that Helen will not leave the hospital. The attorney tells Susan exactly what she must say to Helen in order to ensure that all necessary information has been communicated in a legal manner.

Susan approaches Helen and repeats what the attorney has instructed her to say: that refusing an assignment is insubordination, that insubordination is punishable by suspension and/or termination, and that Helen must leave the hospital and not return to work until after she has met with the Director of Nursing on Monday. Helen, now very upset and afraid for her job, says that she will reconsider working in ICU.

Susan has grown increasingly angry and annoyed with Helen, but she now becomes conciliatory. She tells Helen that she feels very bad about what has happened, but that another nurse is coming to work in ICU and Helen is not needed either there or in her regularly scheduled unit.

Helen then hands Susan a letter signed by herself, Sarah Williams, and Catherine Tanney. The letter states that Helen is unqualified to work in ICU and that assigning her there is unfair to her and unsafe for patient care. Helen then leaves the hospital.

On Monday morning, the Director of Nursing meets with Susan to review the situation. When it is time for her meeting with the Director, Helen appears with a union representative and informs the Director that she and the union consider this meeting Step Two of the grievance procedure. (Ordinarily, the grievance procedure starts with Step One, an informational meeting at which a preliminary effort is made to resolve differences.)

∾o∾

INSTRUCTIONS AND QUESTIONS

You, the Director of Nursing, are aware of the impact your decision will have on the upcoming contract negotiations between the union and Associated Hospitals. If your decision is favorable to the union, the union representatives will demand that the individual employees be allowed to decide the limits of their professional competency and to override management decisions regarding staffing. The union will also attempt to formalize this by making it a part of the proposed contract.

1. Discuss the ramifications of any decisions you will make.
2. How will the decision affect the hospital association's bargaining position?
3. Whatever decision you make no doubt will be appealed by Helen and will result in binding arbitration. Does this have any effect on your decision?
4. If the arbitrator reverses your decision on appeal, what effect will this have on upcoming negotiations?

You also must consider the way in which the situation developed. You believe that Susan acted in an abrupt and overly authoritarian manner and backed Helen into a corner. Helen is a good and well-intentioned nurse who has been receiving a great deal of pressure from the union. On the other hand, you believe that management must have the right to make decisions regarding staffing.

Should you take action against any other persons involved in this case?

PART TWO

Ethical and Personal Dilemmas

		Page
8.	A Zealous City Employee	53
9.	AIDS Patients	58
10.	Ann's Dilemma	60
11.	A Case of Bureaucratic Morality?	63
12.	Anna Lieberman, Deceased	65
13.	One Perspective on Hillsdale Tower	70
14.	The Outsider	78
15.	Thompson's Time Management	82

8

A Zealous City Employee

PART 1

For 16 years, George Wright had worked for Regional City's Traffic Engineering Department, the last five years in parking-meter repair. George and four others in the same shop were each responsible for maintaining about 400 meters. There was talk around the Traffic Engineering shop that the city was considering the removal of all parking meters. They did not seem to be bringing in enough money to justify the hassles they encouraged—merchants who complained that the meters hurt business, spotty enforcement, meters that did not work or had been vandalized, and so on.

If the meters went, George reasoned, he would be out of a job, a job he liked very much. George took pride in his work and was seldom at a loss for opportunities to exercise his skills. In Regional City there were enough broken parking meters to provide George and his fellow workers with all they could handle. Besides routine maintenance and the predictable level of mechanical breakdowns, there were many acts of vandalism of parking meters.

These vandalized meters particularly disturbed George. His interest in his job had always extended beyond mere diligence in repair work. He contemplated ways of reducing the number and seriousness of breakdowns and of increasing shop efficiency. Little could be done to reduce the frequency of occasional mechanical failures, but George felt he could do something about vandalism. With the approval of his superiors, he began staking out blocks of his parking meters at night. Either alone or with Claude Harvey, another veteran in the shop, he would sit in his car for hours, drinking coffee and eating from a brown bag, waiting for would-be vandals to make their move.

His vigilance brought rewards. Several times he spotted a youth or an occasional vagrant attempting to break into one of "his" meters. A quick call to the police typically led to an arrest. As a rule, George's cases were sound enough to result in convictions, and the police appreciated his efforts. He would always call them to make the arrest rather than take any action of his own that might jeopardize chances of obtaining a conviction.

Before continuing reading, what do you do next?

∾o∾

INSTRUCTIONS AND QUESTIONS

1. Evaluate the decision by George's superiors. Were they wise in giving him their approval to stake out the meters? In responding to this question, develop a list of pros and cons of approving such surveillance.
2. At a broader level, how should you treat zealots in public jobs?

PART 2

George began his stake-out program early in the year, shortly after Acme Armored Car Service won its first contract for emptying the city's parking meters. Farrago Armored Service Corporation, which had held the contract for the previous 23 years, had finally been underbid by Acme in December. With the change in collection services, receipts from the meters increased markedly. Farrago collections had ranged from $1,600 to $2,000 a week during the year. Under Acme, receipts were never less than $3,000 a week, reaching a high of $4,048 one week. During the last six months that Farrago held the contract, they had turned in $45,173 to the city. During the same six months a year later, Acme turned $90,000 over to Regional City.

Neither Regional City officials nor Farrago executives could explain this drastic increase in revenues. Variations in weather, traffic, or the amount of vandalism could account for some fluctuations from week to week, but nothing like the consistently higher intake being reported by Acme.

Several points were definite. There had been no substantial increase in the number of meters in operation: During the last six months of their contract, Farrago had collected from an average of 1,863 meters a week, and a year later Acme was collecting from 1,896 meters. Moreover, the last rate increase for meters had been over eight years ago. Nor was there any noticeable increase in traffic or parking in the city during the period when the contract was changing hands. In short, about the same number of meters being used by approximately the same number of cars was suddenly yielding twice the amount of revenue for the city.

Some observers began to speculate that large amounts of "lost revenue" might be involved. Some said $300,000, others estimated $1 million, but only guesses were possible. This year, as well as for the preceding 23 years, meter revenues were one of the few sources of city revenue classified as "unaccountable." The city never actually sees the coins, nor do they audit the collection company's records. The contract is let for bids on the basis of how much the company will charge for emptying each meter and how much the company will charge for processing the coins. Acme had won the contract with a bid of 24 cents per meter and 53 cents per thousand coins. Each meter is emptied once a week, and the coins are sorted, counted, and rolled by machines at the collection company's offices. The company then either deposits the coins in a bank account or sells them to businesses in need of coins. At the end of each week, the city receives a check for the amount collected, and at the end of the month the city pays for the collections.

Before continuing reading, what do you do next?
Put yourself in George's position. What should he do now?

PART 3

The sharp upturn in the city's parking meter income reinforced George's decision about his stake-out program. The mystery of the missing revenues became something of a point of honor with him, and he felt the need to remove all possibility of suspicion directed against himself. As he put it: "If Farrago is saying all they do is collect the money, and nobody is caught taking the money, well then, they are soon going to start saying old George done it."

On the night of June 18, George's heightened vigilance added an explosive new twist to the mystery. George had been staking out a block of meters near County Hospital when, about 10 P.M., a car pulled up in the space behind him. George crouched low in his seat and watched through his outside mirror, spilling his hot coffee. A well-dressed couple emerged from the car. As they stood embracing near a meter George caught sight of the man's arm reaching out and inserting a key into the meter. The meter opened, and the change spilled into the woman's oversized purse. George soon pulled away slowly from the curb and went to find police. Minutes later, he located an officer and alerted him to the situation. The officer moved in and arrested Martin Reed and Ellen Desmond.

According to the arrest report and court records, police found a key ring with nine parking meter keys in Reed's pocket. Desmond's purse contained only nine dimes and ten pennies at the time of the arrest. However, a search of the car turned up a nylon bag filled with about $40 worth of loose change and a glass container with another $17 in rolled coins inside it.

Reed was a Regional City Fire Captain, and his companion was an employee of the U.S. Postal Service. In addition, Reed had worked part time for Farrago for most of the last 23 years. His job, until the firm lost the parking-meter contract, had been to empty parking meters. Apparently, a number of other city police and fire department personnel also had similar moonlighting jobs.

Farrago officials had no immediate explanation for why Reed had a full set of parking-meter keys six months after their contract and his job had been terminated. As Executive Vice President Grimsly Bernard stated, "We only know what we read in the papers. We don't know where Reed got the keys, or even if they are our keys." Bernard later added that there was "no connection between that incident and the man's job with Farrago." After consulting with their parent firm, Farrago officials made one further statement:

> There is no reason to believe, at the present time, that there is any connection between the arrest of a former Farrago employee who had been charged with tampering with a parking meter and the alleged increase in meter collection revenues by a new contracting company.

The rest of the statement suggested that additional revenues might be attributed to other factors, such as an increase in the number of meters, increased parking-meter rates, and increased use of downtown parking space. It added that Farrago would conduct a thorough investigation of its own and would have no further comment, pending the outcome of that investigation. Farrago also announced that it would, in the future, bid on the collection contract, and would continue its practice of employing city personnel as part-time collectors. "What better source of trained and reliable people is there?" a company source asked. "We need people who can take care of themselves in a pinch."

Shortly after his arrest, Reed suggested to city officials that he was being framed and that other unnamed city employees were stealing from the meters. He admitted the keys came from Farrago, but claimed that he had them merely as souvenirs of his long-time job and that they no longer fit most of the city's modern parking meters.

Reed was suspended from the fire department after his arrest, but he was reinstated a few months later. Reed's lawyer filed a motion to suppress all evidence found in Reed's car, on the grounds that the police had conducted an illegal search. The motion was granted, leaving prosecutors with only the $1 found in Desmond's purse as evidence. The county solicitor's office appealed the decision and pledged to prosecute even if their appeal were denied.

∽◦∾

INSTRUCTIONS AND QUESTIONS

You are George Wright, and you try to think through a course of action.

1. What do you do now? What are your fears? What are your reasonable expectations? Do you expect retribution as a "whistle blower"?
2. Consider yourself a city management analyst. Design a system of policies and procedures for meter collection that will prevent such occurrences in the future.

9

AIDS Patients

Jody is the executive director of an AIDS outreach project in a city of 40,000 residents. His agency serves as a clearinghouse for AIDS education and information, acts as an advocate for AIDS patients, and helps place patients in the two hospices located in the city. Eighty percent of the funding for this worthwhile project comes from the city council. Without this support, the project would likely have to close or severely curtail its services. Although independent fundraising activities are slowly picking up, Jody has not been able either to hire a fundraiser or to find time to enlarge the effort himself.

He has learned recently that the ambulance company with which the city government has contracted for all emergency and other patient transport services has been hesitant to transport AIDS patients between doctors' offices, the hospital, and their residences. In fact, he is convinced that ambulance drivers have refused, on occasion, to respond to emergency calls from residences occupied by gay men. He has heard rumors that each driver carries a map with houses known to belong to gays marked with a red X. Despite this information, Jody believes the service is getting better, although he has no way of really knowing other than occasional anecdotal information.

Last month, he reported his suspicions to the city council president and was told in no uncertain terms that any further outcry would result in a serious review of the city's funding of the AIDS project. The city, he was told, had contracted with the same ambulance service for 24 years with very few problems. The service was inexpensive, efficient, and always underbid its competitor. In fact, if it weren't for such cost savings, the council would not be able to fund the AIDS project.

∽o∽
INSTRUCTIONS AND QUESTIONS

1. What would you advise Jody to do, if anything, at this time?
2. What are the competing ethical values involved?
3. What decision-making process would you recommend he use to determine which value should take precedence?

10

Ann's Dilemma

Ann Czaplicki is glad to have any job. She completed enough education courses to be certified as a high school teacher, but her English literature major was not in great demand. So, she became a part-time taxi driver and continued writing poetry, several pieces of which were published in a local magazine.

After a year of this life, a family acquaintance offered Ann a job as his assistant. Harry Goetz is an important official of the state Health Department. His office has a major say in the approval of new health facilities of various kinds, particularly for acute and extended care.

Ann knows little about the health field at first, but she reads a lot and learns fast. In less than a year, she becomes so knowledgeable that Goetz moves her into a program position in which she no longer has any secretarial duties. Ann remains on good terms with Goetz and sees him often, even though she now reports to another person.

Late one afternoon, Goetz's secretary calls Ann and tells her that Goetz would like to see her before she goes home. Ann gets her things together a few minutes early and goes over to his office. Goetz stays on the phone until after his secretary leaves.

Once they are alone, Goetz asks a favor of Ann.

"I have recently gotten information," he begins, "which leads me to believe that one of your co-workers is giving some nursing-home owners and builders advance word on the activities of this office. There is a lot of money that can be made if people have such inside information, Ann, as you know."

Goetz gets to the essential point, quickly. "Ann," he says, "I want you to keep an eye on that person for me."

"I don't want to call in the police, you know, because I'm only reasonably certain. And I don't want to be embarrassed if I am wrong. If my suspicions are confirmed, I'll call in the cops and you'll be out of it entirely, Ann.

"I'll give you the person's name when I have your agreement and your pledge of secrecy."

Ann does not have a chance to respond before Goetz goes further. He softens his voice:

"I know that it may seem that I am asking a lot, Ann, but I'm going to presume on our relationship even further. I would really appreciate it if you would go through that person's desk, preferably today, before you go home. I'm pretty sure that you will find some notes or correspondence that will confirm what I suspect."

"Gee, Mr. Goetz," Ann replies, "I've never done anything like that before."

"I understand, Ann," Goetz responds. "That's why I know I can rely on you to help. I feel I have been very good to you: I gave you some breaks that many other people, with better qualifications on paper, would have been eager to get. This is one way that you can repay those favors and, at the same time, help put a stop to some practices that we both abhor."

"I appreciate what you have done for me, Mr. Goetz," Ann responds. "But I still feel a little funny about going through someone's desk. Besides, I wasn't planning to go back to my office this evening: The janitorial people are already in there sweeping. Can I think about this overnight? I really do want to help you out."

"Why don't you do that, Ann," Goetz says. "Remember that you may help put a stop to some of the most unscrupulous operations in this business.

"I know you'll make the right decision. After you think about it, you will see that this is a fair way to recognize the breaks I've given you and can continue to give you."

∽o∾

INSTRUCTIONS AND QUESTIONS

You are Ann, and your head is spinning. Goetz has put you on the spot—his continued favor seems conditional on your doing something that is of doubtful legality, that is personally repugnant to you, and that may not be easy to stop once you start.

Goetz's request is too much like the kind of end-justifies-the-means morality you protested about in college. And you also feel there is an element of personal exploitation involved.

But Goetz has been good to you, and you like your job. So, you initially wrestle with two alternatives.

First, you can agree to do the job. The problem there is that you can only guess which of several people Goetz has in mind. One of the possibilities is a young man with whom you are beginning to make friends.

Second, you can go back to Goetz the next day and tell him that you have decided not to honor his request. When he asks why, you will say that you appreciate and respect the trust he has in you. But if you were to go through someone's desk for him, you will explain to Goetz, he can never be sure that you would not go through *his* desk for someone else at another time.

You are Ann. Evaluate the two options. On analysis, do other options occur to you? What do you decide?

11

A Case of Bureaucratic Morality?

Dr. John R. Heller, Chief of the U.S. Health Service's Venereal Disease Division, held overall responsibility for an experimental syphilis study that he developed years earlier in Macon County, Alabama.* The objective of the longitudinal experimental health study was to determine the effects of syphilis on the human body. The experiment was based on a sample of African-American males (N=600) who were primarily poor and uneducated. Four hundred men diagnosed with syphilis in the Tuskegee area were recruited for the experimental group. Two hundred men who did not have the venereal disease were assigned to the control group. The 400 men already affected with the disease in the experimental group would not receive any treatment. They would, however, receive examinations and treatment periodically for any other maladies they might have, except for the syphilis itself. When the men in both the experimental and control groups died, an autopsy would be performed for comparison purposes. The autopsy would determine the actual cause of death and help establish incidence rates between the control group and the experimental group.

When the Tuskegee Health Experiment first began in 1932, penicillin was not in use. Standard treatment for syphilis consisted primarily of prescribing highly toxic drugs such as arsenic and mercury. Most physi-

*See "The Tuskegee Health Experiment: A Question of Bureaucratic Morality?" by Walter D. Broadnax, *The Bureaucrat* Vol. 4, No. 1 (April 1975), pp. 45–55, and the *New York Times*, July 26, 28, August 8, 9, 1972, for additional information.

cians, however, opted not to treat the disease, rather than to use these toxic drugs. Penicillin was perfected 10 years later, roughly at the same time Dr. Heller became Chief of the U.S. Health Service's Venereal Disease Division.

In 1966, Peter Buxton, a former employee of the U.S. Public Health Service, raised the issue of the morality of the federal syphilis study. Two years later, the Centers for Disease Control issued a written response whereby Mr. Buxton was informed that "the decision not to treat the patients had been made on the basis of their ages. Massive penicillin therapy could have serious side effects on the patients, and furthermore, the disease was now dormant in the surviving participants" (*New York Times*, 1972: 43).

The Tuskegee Health Experiment became a crisis in morality and ethics for the federal bureaucracy only when the case became public in 1972. An Associated Press (AP) correspondent discovered the story while covering the 1972 Democratic Convention in Miami, Florida.

∽ॐ∽

INSTRUCTIONS AND QUESTIONS

1. What are the moral and ethical issues that this case presents?
2. The Tuskegee case can be viewed as an example of a moral and ethical decision made by the federal bureaucracy. Do definitions of what is ethical and moral change as persons, times, and situations change?
3. Obviously, problems of ethics and morality can, and frequently do, occur each day in an administrative setting. Could you, as an administrator, at any time justify actions that you might feel were morally or ethically wrong? Explain your stand and discuss its impact upon the administrative process.

12

Anna Lieberman, Deceased

Alan Buchner has been combating discrimination for many years, and the recent death of Anna Lieberman again forces him to confront his own values and to decide what he should do. He reviews, painfully, his history and that of Anna.

A veteran of civil-rights marches from the earliest days, Buchner was interested in the plight of the elderly years before it became fashionable. He held a number of responsible positions in the social-service agencies of his community, most recently as director of an extended-care facility that was recognized around the state for its innovative programming. Buchner was active in professional societies and in meetings of "concerned citizens." He organized, and still chairs, a leading local citizen-advocate group for the elderly. Although regarded by his friends and followers as dedicated, professional, efficient, and extremely competent, he is criticized by those less fond of him. His critics find Buchner ideological, often tactless though effective, and generally involved in too many projects to do justice to all of them. Buchner recently was hired as the director of an experimental program for the mentally retarded.

Local community care for the retarded is not well financed. There is sufficient local and state funding for institutionally maintaining dependent people, but there is little left for either clinical or vocational programs. Buchner was hopeful that, if his program showed some success, it might open the door for better funding of similar experiments and perhaps even change community attitudes toward the elderly and retarded.

Buchner's new job involves managing a halfway house for retarded adults who have been institutionalized for many years. If such people can be brought more into community life, Buchner reasoned, then other institutionalized people might later get a similar opportunity. In a halfway house, there are only two or three people to a room. These "clients" can leave the house with freedom, go out to shop, or go for a walk. Clients there get closer, more personal attention than in a regular mental institution where the "patients" or even "inmates" are often kept in large wards with many beds, eat institution food at long tables, and, during the day, sit in the "day room" attached to their ward when not receiving some kind of treatment.

Buchner's halfway house employs several unit leaders, each of whom works with several client groups. A client group is composed of two to four clients plus an equal number of therapy aides and service coordinators. In addition, there is a staff of advocates who are supposed to protect the rights of the clients with respect to professional treatment, in client dealings with other members of the staff of the halfway house, and in their relationships with people outside the halfway house.

Buchner is able to recruit a dedicated staff composed largely of people who came to know him in his previous professional or community activities. But, one problem Buchner has not been able to solve is that of medical services for the clients. The halfway house needs a contractual, prepaid group arrangement for medical services that will assure comprehensive and timely care of the clients' needs.

Buchner's successes and failures are both patent in the case of Anna Lieberman. Anna came to the halfway house after virtually a lifetime in institutional settings. She was first placed in a private institution for children at the age of three. Anna's parents died when she was 15. Anna's older sister was her closest friend, and she cared for Anna and financially supported her. But when Anna was 25, her sister was killed in an automobile accident. Under the management of the state, Anna's inheritance from her sister lasted only two years. At 27, lack of money forced her out of the private children's facility and into a state institution. Two years later, she was accused of having sexual relations with a male client at the institution. After she was involuntarily sterilized, Anna was confined in a locked ward for the severely retarded and multiple handicapped. The 60 beds in the ward were so close together that Anna had to climb over five beds just to get to her own.

Upon returning to her original ward after two years, Anna was socially detached and unresponsive. She spent most of her time sitting in a chair against the wall, staring into space. The only major variation was when her one friend, another client, came to sit and talk with her. In this institution, no one left the sitting room unless accompanied by an attendant. The ward itself included only 25 beds, reasonably spaced, and was therefore an improvement over the locked ward in which Anna was kept for two years. Formal education was never provided for Anna.

At 59, Anna was moved again, at state initiative, to participate in an experimental project aimed at "deinstitutionalizing" those who had been in an institutional setting for extended periods. Although she had to leave her friend, only the second she ever made, Anna's new placement had major advantages.

Anna shared a bath with only one other client and a kitchen with several others. She was given a thorough evaluation, from which it was concluded that the 59-year-old Anna was functioning at a 9-year-old level and tested at a 12-year-old level. Anna was compliant and was considered to be badly atrophied socially. This was not surprising to the staff at the new institution, for they had seen many cases in which clients suffered impairment of their ability to function even though their intellectual performance remained stable.

The staff developed a progress and treatment plan for Anna, the aim of which was to help Anna help herself in her own development. It took Anna over a year and a half to adjust to this new environment. Her previous history made it difficult for her to respond in this strange new setting where neither corporal punishment nor behavior-modifying drugs nor restraining devices were employed routinely.

At the halfway house managed by Buchner, to which Anna was next transferred when the staff considered her ready, she made slow but continued progress. She accepted her new independence, assumed more personal responsibility, and demonstrated less fear of the consequences of her action. The halfway house was small enough, and Alan Buchner's hours were long enough, for him to come to know all the clients well. Anna developed a friendship with Alan and with Kathy Ammons, her advocate. Buchner dug into Anna's history and discovered the details of the conditions in which she lived for so long. Kathy Ammons and Anna took a liking to each other immediately and soon developed a feeling of trust for each other.

Since Anna was over 60 and one of the oldest clients in the halfway house, Kathy paid close attention to Anna's health. Kathy fought for regular examinations for Anna and, when indicated, for proper treatment of her friend's ills.

One Tuesday evening in December, while Kathy was visiting, Anna complained of feeling hot and having a pain in her stomach. Kathy immediately took her to the emergency room at the nearest hospital. It took three-and-a-half hours of waiting and a heated argument before

Anna was seen by a physician. He took her temperature, checked her blood pressure, prescribed a laxative, and released her. Kathy tried unsuccessfully to have her admitted to the hospital.

On Wednesday morning, Anna felt no better. Kathy went to Alan and told him of the previous evening's events. Together they were able to get Anna admitted to the hospital late Wednesday afternoon. She was placed under the care of Dr. Stevenson, one of the several physicians sharing responsibilities for "charity patients." Dr. Stevenson enjoys a community-wide reputation as a surgeon and has the political advantage of having a brother in elective state office. Although Anna had lost fluids as a result of vomiting and the laxatives, Dr. Stevenson did not start treatment to replace these fluids. He gave Anna aspirin, which stabilized her temperature at 102 degrees, but no other medication. Her situation, if not improved, was not obviously deteriorating.

On Friday morning, Buchner went to an out-of-town meeting after stopping at the hospital to see Anna. Two hours after he departed, she went into a coma. Kathy spent most of the day trying to reach Buchner. Dr. Stevenson continued his treatment and responded to Kathy's doubts with a reaffirmation of his diagnosis that Anna was suffering from an intestinal blockage that soon would clear up.

Buchner returned Saturday evening, picked up Kathy on his way from the airport, and they went directly to the hospital to see Anna. The nurse on duty told them that Anna's condition was stable though she remained in a coma.

Early Sunday morning, Anna died. The autopsy report stated that the primary cause of death was a massive infection resulting from a ruptured appendix and compounded by dehydration.

After reading the autopsy report, Buchner sought out Dr. Stevenson at the hospital. "Why wasn't she given fluids? Why wasn't her illness diagnosed properly? This woman never should have died for these reasons," he charged.

Stevenson seemed annoyed but answered calmly. "Mr. Buchner, as a physician my concern is with patients with a future. This patient hardly had a past, never mind a future. Every day I treat patients who have productive lives that are interrupted by illness, and every day I know that somewhere there is the life of a productive, contributing person that I might have saved if the day were an hour longer. I have no time for the losers.

"You call yourself an advocate," Stevenson continued. "Why don't you go out and advocate for the lives of the winners who need care? I think sometimes that people like yourself are as much losers as the pitiful beings you preserve."

Buchner could not contain his anger and snarled: "Do you know that this autopsy report alone is probable grounds for malpractice? I won't stoop to discuss the ethics of that charming speech you just gave."

"I don't think you could find a medical board or a court in this state that would let that hold up," Stevenson retorted. A trace of a smile crossed his face. "Perhaps you have forgotten who I am?"

"The question is more *what* you are," Buchner snapped and abruptly left.

∽o∽

INSTRUCTIONS AND QUESTIONS

Alan faces a dilemma. If he decides to initiate proceedings against the physician, Stevenson can counter with political pressures. At worst, this might jeopardize the entire halfway-house program.

Because of Stevenson's position in the medical profession, initiating proceedings probably also would decrease the likelihood of securing acceptable prepaid contractual medical services at the hospital for the halfway house.

Either outcome would be a setback for the advocates of quality care for the retarded and the elderly as well as for the movement for deinstitutionalization that they represent.

Failure to prosecute allows Stevenson to continue practicing his brand of medicine to the likely detriment of other patients like Anna. It also may be read as tacit support for that kind of care by other physicians with similar views. Failure to prosecute also implies serious moral issues for Buchner.

You are Buchner:

1. What would you do about the death of Anna Lieberman?
2. Now think about the case as one of interorganizational relations. What are the characteristics of the relations between the hospital and the halfway house?
3. Can you come up with a strategy for developing a relation with the hospital that would better meet the needs of the clients of the halfway house?

13

One Perspective on Hillsdale Tower

If there is one human around whom the personality of an airport control tower can be centered, it is the Chief Controller, who commands a tremendous amount of authority and responsibility. Three of the major goals of a tower for which the Chief has overall responsibility are: (1) maintenance of the best possible relations with outside interests; (2) provision for high-caliber air-traffic service to a wide clientele; and (3) operation of the facility, which in this case is a control tower with radar-approach control service.

This story describes one way of handling these multiple goals in a very specific place.

The problems at Hillsdale Tower basically resulted from an imbalance in emphasis among the three major goals above. On the one hand, the imbalance brings accolades for the facility from many of the external interests, including the flying public. On the other hand, much dissatisfaction and bickering exists among the facility personnel.

Hillsdale Tower lies at the center of a dynamic and progressive region and controls a significant flow of people and products. From a modern four-story brick structure, air traffic arriving or departing within a 40-mile radius of the airport is controlled or assisted using the most modern surveillance radar. Atop the building is the tower "cab" from which local airport traffic is directed.

No one can forget for very long why Hillsdale came to be what it is. Unusually friendly people who cooperated more than average—that was Hillsdale's successful combination. Even new arrivals in Hillsdale learn that lesson, fast! Local boosters—especially economic notables and those with a direct interest in continued expansion—trumpet the gospel in friendly but persistent ways.

The federal employees at Hillsdale Tower learn the lesson as well as anybody; some experience directly how a culture can mobilize major forces to influence even the unwilling.

A BRIEF OVERVIEW: ADVANCING BY WORKING YOURSELF DOWNWARD

Unlike most office buildings, in which the new employee starts a career on the lower floors and works toward the top floors, employees in Hillsdale Tower start at the top and work downward as they progress. After preliminary training, employees typically start their on-the-job training in the tower cab, a glass-enclosed cage located on the fourth floor. All of the airport landings and take-offs are directed from this vantage point. The cab also receives clearances and instructions from the radar room and relays them to aircraft.

On the third floor is the radar room, technically called the TRACON (Terminal Radar Control) Room. All of the radar services provided by the facility originate in this room using Airport Surveillance Radar (ASR-4) equipment. The room is equipped with adjustable lighting; acoustical ceiling, walls, and floor; and air conditioning and heating. These features make working conditions tenable in the noisy and darkened room. Also located on this floor are the training rooms, rest rooms, lunch room, and various equipment and supply rooms.

The second floor houses most of the electronic gear necessary for the facility.

On the first floor are located the offices of the top FAA officials in the building: the Chief Controller of the tower and the Chief of Systems Maintenance.

Finally, the basement houses the heating and air-conditioning systems for the building, along with a Civil Defense Bomb Shelter.

FAA air-traffic–control facilities are strictly regulated by numerous manuals and publications promulgated by Washington Headquarters, as interpreted by the regional office and as precisely defined by facility chiefs. These manuals include the *Facility Operations Manual*, which specifies how a facility should be operated; and the *Air Traffic Control Procedure Manual*, which defines the rules and procedures necessary for the uniform control of air traffic.

Position	No.	Responsibilities
Chief Controller	1	Overall operation of the tower; high-caliber service to wide clientele; maintenance of good relations with outside interests.
Secretary	1	Under supervision of Chief Controller.
Watch Supervisors	4	Operation of tower on assigned shift; collateral staff duties as assigned by Chief Controller.
Coordinators	3	Operation of TRACON on assigned shift under general supervision of Watch Supervisor.
Controllers	15	Any assigned position of operation; overall operation of tower cab when so assigned.
Assistant	2	Flight data position; other positions under supervision of controller.
Total Positions	26	

Hillsdale Tower is staffed with 26 personnel who, for the most part, rotate on shifts (see accompanying table). This enables the facility to operate around the clock 365 days a year.

Internal Relations: Open Door or Trap Door?

Newcomers, upon arriving at Hillsdale Tower, are impressed with the advertised "open door" policy for the Chief. However, after submitting a few suggestions for improvement of the facility they see a different pattern. They seldom receive an actual *no* but also seldom receive a *yes*. Eventually, they find that only by exerting extreme pressure will they force a specific decision. Although they may believe they have won a victory in such cases, more often, employees eventually realize through small insinuations that they have gone too far and should not have "rocked the boat" in the first place. For those who miss such messages, Hillsdale also has a record of silent retribution, primarily in the form of mediocre promotion appraisals and performance ratings. The "open door" can be a "trap door," in short.

The overall climate at Hillsdale is usually attractive and yet sometimes induces despair. The giving of orders at Hillsdale is extremely rare, which suggests pleasantness and easy consensus, which is often the case. But order-giving is rare because supervisory personnel tend to feel that their orders will not be backed up. This induces despair, especially for the employees who believe that something needs to be done and soon. For example, a training officer prepared a test for facility personnel. When one person refused to take the test, nothing happened; the next time several persons refused to take the test, still nothing happened. The training officer gave up and, for years after that, there was no training program at the facility.

Newcomers eventually learn that this "trap door" policy applies to all facility operations whether internal or external, including dealings with the regional office in Plains City. Any internal disaffection tends to be localized. For example, the regional office has never conducted a formal evaluation of Hillsdale Tower during the Chief's tenure—apparently because of its highly positive reputation with external clients.

There is a further effective deterrent to organized internal "boat rocking" in Hillsdale Tower. Although the regional office strongly encourages frequent meetings in order to exchange views and to air misunderstandings, such meetings are seldom held at Hillsdale. Since all operational personnel rotate on different shifts and in an irregular way, there is very little opportunity to develop group ties in more informal ways.

External Relations: Group Norms

The Chief Controller also has a definite style in his contacts with clients external to his organization. For example, a violation of regulations should generate a formal charge for the alleged violation in accordance with published FAA procedures. The way procedure is interpreted at Hillsdale, a report is filed only as a last resort, which generally means that another external client has been involved in the incident and insists that a report be filed.

Clients could not ask for a more compatible arrangement. Pilots can count on complete cooperation from the tower, including special handling in many cases. Many of them get away with violations even when they fully expect the book to be thrown at them. For example, one airline pilot reported in at the wrong altitude. Upon arriving at the airport, the pilot speedily called the tower to admit his mistake. When he was informed that no other traffic was involved and that no report would be filed, he was most grateful, for he well knew that, had the incident been reported, he would probably have received a fine. Although this procedure is also not by the book, it has made friends for Hillsdale Tower. On occasion, it also has benefited some of the controllers who have their mistakes overlooked.

Tower personnel are pulled in two ways, consequently. They find deep satisfaction in their ability to provide superior service to external clients, but they are often frustrated in their efforts to go beyond the call of duty on internal matters. Because of group norms, not only do they fail to receive encouragement from their Chief, but they also gain the scorn of many of the tower personnel who let them know rather bluntly that they do not like "show-offs." This atmosphere naturally does not support those who desire to do more than the minimum work. But they usually accept the group norm, work their eight-hour shifts, and go home.

ADMINISTRATIVE PROCESS: SOME SUMMARY CHARACTERIZATIONS

The following description of Hillsdale's administrative process provides a more detailed look at Hillsdale's problem.

Communications

In a formal structure, one would expect minutes to be taken at staff meetings held between the Chief and the Watch Supervisors. At Hillsdale, there are no such written records. Consequently, a revised procedure agreed upon in a meeting might be interpreted differently by each supervisor. This on occasion creates confusion on the part of air-traffic controllers, who are told different ways to function with no written instructions to clear up the situation.

Performance Evaluation

One of the more serious problems that exist within the facility is that personnel are not informed of their weaknesses. There are extreme cases in which the Chief will not take corrective action—even after being informed by supervisors that individuals are not doing acceptable work.

Performance Ratings and Promotion Appraisals

Another distinct feature of Hillsdale Tower is its approach to handling performance ratings and promotion appraisals. Although instructions from regional headquarters in Plains City require that these forms be discussed with the individual concerned, this was not done at Hillsdale until recently. This put the individual in the position of not knowing for sure where he or she stood. All personnel were officially considered to be doing good work, regardless of whether they were or not. The philosophy seemed to be that it is better to give "satisfactory" ratings to all personnel rather than risk morale problems that might be created by giving unsatisfactory or outstanding ratings to a few people. One result of this procedure was that in 10 years no one had been promoted to a major job outside the facility.

PATTERNS OF POWER AND CONFLICT: SOME SUMMARY CHARACTERIZATIONS

Hillsdale Tower is characterized by the following patterns of power and conflict.

Cooperation

Newcomers soon learn that they are expected to subjugate personal feelings in the interest of cooperation with external interests, which are quite powerful. The system of internal cooperation ensures that personnel make no serious waves. Consequently, conditions will be quite pleasant, for the most part.

Conflict

A major policy of the facility is to avoid conflict with all external clients, especially those who might cause repercussions. Therefore, newcomers learn that, since they are public servants, they will often have to take abuse rather than enter into confrontation or conflict with an external client. This policy is very effective in one sense, but it causes serious dissatisfaction for those who have to swallow their pride or their sense of what is professionally appropriate.

Internal conflict centers around a generalized resistance to change. This situation results in a serious inner conflict for some facility personnel, because they are placed in the frustrating position of having even their most ambitious ideas ignored.

Another source of conflict stems from the fact that during the 1940s and 1950s, the typical FAA manager had no more preparation for the job than the experience of coming up through the ranks as a technician. The prevailing concept was that the best way to learn about government management is to work at it. In the 1950s, the FAA sought to improve its management in what proved to be a puzzling way. Managerial training was given mainly to the lower levels of supervision, and almost none was given to middle-management levels and above. This resulted in the situation of having many first-line supervisors more eager to employ modern management techniques than their supervisors. Very often, this disparity created resentment and resistance on the part of the subordinates. Fortunately, the FAA spotted this source of conflict and revised its thinking.

Another source of conflict related to the problem of training is that the grade structure of the agency places only the best technicians in the higher grades and thereby makes them the only ones eligible to bid on high-paying management jobs. The agency is attempting to rectify this problem by placing greater emphasis on supervisory characteristics on the promotion appraisal forms.

Search for Equilibrium

Fortunately, the new management training efforts of the agency have begun to show dividends at Hillsdale, and some of the sources of conflict have very recently disappeared. Basically, there is a growing realization that it is necessary at Hillsdale to satisfy internal clients as well as external clients. For example, performance ratings are now discussed with personnel by the training officer, who is one of the Watch Supervisors.

Delegated Responsibilities

Little responsibility is delegated to other supervisory personnel except in training, and, even there, delegation is quite limited. Delegated responsibilities are often unclearly defined or overlapping, moreover, so that it is quite difficult to pin down supervisory or staff duties. For example, individuals were given operational problems to work on without the knowledge of the Operations Officer. This naturally discouraged the Operations Officer from attempting to develop his position into a meaningful power base. Possibly, this is just what the Chief wants.

Inaction Is Power

Another source of power for the Chief is his expert use of the pocket veto, his decision not to act. This can be a very powerful tool.

Leaving Well Enough Alone

As long as external clients continue to praise the facility and as long as the regional office leaves it alone, there is no credible reason for facility personnel to resist the system. The scales are tipped so far in the direction of external client satisfaction that little weight is given to internal dissatisfaction.

AGENCY GOALS MET IN SPITE OF INTERNAL CONFLICT

Thus, a paradoxical situation exists at Hillsdale Tower. On the one hand, hidden internal conflict exists between the Chief and those facility personnel who feel that the facility is close to collapse. Their interests are unsatisfied, and their efficiency is not what it could be. They often cause tension and internal dissension to spread, creating some dissatisfaction among others.

On the other hand, the facility supplies superior service to the external clients. The controllers and resource suppliers in the regional office are happy. Clients are more than satisfied by what they consider service of above-average helpfulness and courtesy. Whatever his other characteristics, it is clear that the Chief is effective in meeting overall goals, at least in the short run.

∽◦∽

INSTRUCTIONS AND QUESTIONS

You have a staff responsibility for supervisory development at the regional level. Your visit to Hillsdale leaves you somewhat troubled. You wish the Chief Controller were more active in developing his subordinates; but you do not want to jeopardize the positive aspects of Hillsdale's performance.

1. What do you do?
2. Detail the various factors or forces that you see creating the present situation at Hillsdale.
3. Which are most central?
4. Which might you be able to change without detracting from day-to-day performance?

14

The Outsider

Bill Wilson has recently been hired as Supervising Programmer for the Polk County Data Processing Department. Prior to taking this position, he worked as system analyst for one of the major accounting and management consulting firms. Two years ago this firm was awarded a large contract to completely revamp Polk County's cost accounting and management information system (MIS), and Wilson had been part of the project team assigned to the job. The system programming and installation had gone very smoothly, and Wilson had acquired a reputation as a "super" programmer and troubleshooter. He had also made several good friends among the county employees, including Frank Sullivan, the Assistant County Executive and the county's MIS project manager, and Jim Duncan, a gifted young programming analyst.

Wilson had not been taken completely by surprise, then, when he received a call from Frank Sullivan informing him of an opening and encouraging him to apply. But when Wilson was eventually offered the job, he was not sure whether he wanted it. Although the position paid only about the same as his current one, it did provide the opportunity to move into management and to coordinate group efforts, something he was looking for. And, Wilson was tired of the travel and the pressure to conform socially that went along with his present job.

Two things bothered Wilson about taking this new position. He would be coming from outside the agency to take a job for which several department personnel had unsuccessfully competed. This might affect his future working relationships with the staff. The second bothersome item was Wilson's doubt about the capabilities of most of the people he would be supervising. He had worked with several of them on the MIS project and, with the exception of Jim Duncan, had been unimpressed. They had seemed technically unsophisticated in many ways, and so unmotivated that Wilson knew he would probably have to make an extra effort to get anything worthwhile out of them.

What finally convinced him to accept the position was the fact that the head of the Data Processing Department had already announced his plans to take an early retirement in 15 months. Wilson was promised that, if he performed successfully, he would be in line for the department head's job.

Wilson would have liked a little time to get to know his staff, to evaluate their individual capabilities, and to form some positive working relationships before being hit with any major projects. But it did not work out that way. At this morning's staff meeting, the department head announces that Congress just passed legislation imposing a uniform set of financial reporting requirements on all transit districts that receive Urban Mass Transportation Administration (UMTA) funding. The chart of accounts outlined in these requirements is significantly different from the one used by Polk County's transit district, and the virtually new accounting system will have to be reprogrammed to make it conform. Furthermore, the legislation requires that the data be captured in the new breakdowns beginning the next fiscal year, which leaves only about 12 weeks to make the necessary programming changes. Failure to comply would jeopardize the continuing receipt of some $24 million a year in UMTA funding. Wilson has no choice but to forge ahead and hope for the best.

He starts by roughing out the overall system design, and then breaks the project into tasks, which he distributes to his five senior programmers. Each programmer will be responsible for working on a section of the overall plan, after which the finished work will be pieced together to form the complete system. Wilson decides that, to demonstrate the confidence he has in his staff, he will limit his role to planning, coordinating, and managing the project, and to participating in the actual programming only when it is better to provide a general outline of what is needed than to swamp people with details, especially in the beginning.

At the initial project management meeting, Wilson gives each programmer an overview of what the modified system is intended to accomplish, along with a somewhat more detailed explanation of their individual work assignments. Beyond that point, Wilson feels, the real specifics should become self-evident to each programmer as he or she goes along. He always found that to be true in his own work, at least, and sees no reason why it shouldn't be the same with other experienced programmers.

Wilson schedules another meeting in two weeks to check on the progress of the programmers' work.

In the interim, Wilson is very busy finishing up some other, minor projects in order to concentrate fully on this one, and he does not have a chance to informally check the progress of his programmers. Also, he doesn't want to give them the impression that he is breathing down their necks. The programmers had studied the work intently and asked only a few questions when he assigned it, so Wilson feels comfortable that the project is moving along smoothly.

Once the next meeting begins, Wilson learns, much to his dismay, that the work is not going at all well. Apparently, the other programmers had interpreted the project as a very straightforward coding exercise and were not picking up on the real subtleties of the work as he had expected them to. The result is that their work has barely scratched the surface, and two precious weeks have been virtually wasted.

The project schedule was tight before, and Wilson seriously questions whether it is now even possible to meet the deadline. Wilson knows that the timely completion of the project is critical, and that his new superiors will be watching carefully to see how well he handles this first important assignment.

As he quickly ponders his next move, possible explanations for this alarming turn of events and alternative solutions for this problem race through Wilson's mind. The people he chose for this project are the most experienced in his group and they should have been able to handle the work with the directions he gave them. Since they did not, the reason must be either that they didn't care or that they are challenging him as their new supervisor. Under the circumstances, it appears necessary to tell them pointedly that he doesn't like what's going on and that he is going to make life very uncomfortable until each task is done properly.

Since Wilson badly wants to assume the best about his new staff, he could approach the situation as though the programmers simply misunderstood what he wanted because his instructions were not specific enough. Although time is very short and it's clear that he will now have to keep a close eye on the project every step of the way, he will have them start over and will work closely with them on an individual basis until the system is completed.

To ensure that the project is completed correctly and on schedule, Wilson can handle a major portion of it himself. After all, he is more familiar with the system that anyone else because of his participation in the original installation, and his own work schedule looks pretty clear for the next 10 weeks. In addition, he will pull Jim Duncan out of the ranks to help. Wilson knows that he can count on Duncan's work and cooperation.

Wilson has serious doubts about whether the project can be completed on schedule using only his own people, regardless of how he approaches them. And it won't look good to higher management if he fails on his first assignment. It would be best, therefore, to see the department head, explain that the programmers he has inherited are not capable enough at this stage to handle such a complex job, and recommend that the hardest parts of the job be contracted out while his staff does the easier portions.

To reassure the department head, Wilson will propose that, once this immediate project is completed, he will institute an intensive training program to bring the staff up to snuff for future projects. Although this would overspend the department's professional services budget and thus require some substantial cutbacks in other areas, it can be justified when one considers the potential financial loss involved.

∽o∾

INSTRUCTIONS AND QUESTIONS

You are Bill Wilson. Because of the importance of the project, you have promised to keep the department head fully informed of all developments. You know that a lot will be riding on your next move.

1. Considering the impact on working relationships with your staff and their future productivity, as well as the impression you will leave with your higher management, what are the advantages and disadvantages of contracting out the hardest parts of the project?
2. In reviewing your own actions to date, can you find fault with any of them?
3. What course of action do you choose, and how should you present it to the department head and to your staff?

15

Thompson's Time Management

John Thompson sank into his office chair, spun around 180 degrees, and looked out the window. "There's got to be a better way of managing my time. I'm stressed to the limit, and now my boss wants this 'rush' report in two days. If I don't change soon, I'm likely to have a heart attack or a nervous breakdown." It was 5:00 P.M. on a Tuesday. John decided to "take stock" of his situation, so he called his wife, Mary, told her that he would be a half-hour late, and started reflecting.

PERSONAL AND PROFESSIONAL BACKGROUND

At age 38, John Thompson was relatively successful compared to many of his high school classmates. He had earned his undergraduate degree in accounting with about a "B" average at the state university. He was married and had two children, ages 9 and 12. His wife, Mary, worked part-time as a nurse, which helped pay for the mortgage on their comfortable house in the suburbs.

After trying to pass the certified public accounting exams, he decided that a governmental job was perhaps a better "fit." Thus, he joined the financial management services of a large state agency, the Department of Human Services. His first job was as an accounts payable clerk. Subsequently, he was promoted to accounts payable supervisor, and after a few lateral shifts, to accounting supervisor.

The accounting function in the Department of Human Services was relatively decentralized. Most departments were quite large and handled their own accounting transactions. Budget approvals and financing were handled at the director's level. John's area handled the day-to-day accounts payable, accounts receivable, bank accounts, payroll, and cash flow for the department. As well, John was responsible for compiling the monthly financial statements and the annual budgets. Five people reported directly to John, and another six people worked as accounting clerks.

As John reflected on his personal and professional background, he thought, "Not so bad for a 'grinder' like me. Things are pretty solid. If only the state paid me 10 percent more to compensate for all of my overtime and job stress."

CHANGES OVER TIME

John had an office with a large desk and a large window. He looked around his office and reflected on the past day, past week, and past six years during which he had had this office and the job as accounting supervisor. Not much had changed. The setting was much the way he found it. The day-to-day discussions and problems were much the same. In fact, most of his time management problems were similar to his first job in financial management services, similar to when he was at the university, and similar to his high school days.

INTERRUPTIONS

John's person-to-person verbal transactions were predictable. Now that he thought about it, interruptions were one of his major time management problems and generators of stress. Typically, John would be settling in to write a report when he would be interrupted. There were about a dozen daily "business" interruptions with supervisors and clerks coming by to ask questions about coding or handling a particular transaction. These took only about five minutes each, but each threw off John's concentration.

Then there were all those "social" interruptions. John thought that there were at least eight daily social interruptions, for about 5 to 30 minutes each. Most were predictable. For example, Fran, the payroll clerk supervisor, would drop by to talk about her marital problems. Sean, the associate director of the department, would find a reason to drop by to talk about his children who studied music and played sports with John and Mary's children.

Jack, the operations manager, was another good example of predictable discussion. As John reflected, a typical conversation would be as follows:

JACK: Hey, did you see that Monday night NFL football game?
JOHN: Yes, did you?
JACK: Yeah.
JOHN: Wasn't that something? Boy, those X's really came through when it counted.

TELEPHONES, FAXES, AND E-MAIL

As if the interruptions from people weren't enough, there were about 10 faxes, 25 E-mail messages, and 15 phone calls each day. At least John could control when he responded to the faxes and the E-mail messages, but the phone calls were a different matter. The phone calls came primarily when John was out of his office at a meeting or trying to fulfill his personal commitment to management-by-walking-around (MBWA). John's secretary, Karen, dutifully took down the caller's name and phone number, while ticking off "please call" on the preprinted telephone call forms. When John returned the calls, the other person usually was not in, and a frustrating game of telephone tennis ensued.

MEETINGS

Preplanned meetings accounted for about 12 hours per week of John's typical 45-hour week. Turning over the daily pages of his desk calendar, John drew up a one-page summary of last week's planned meetings, as follows:

Monday	10:00 A.M.	Meet with staff to discuss need for a new computer software program.
	2:00 P.M.	Meet with supervisor to discuss annual reports and new software costs.
Tuesday	9:30 A.M.	Meet with associate director on changing the monthly reporting format.
	11:30 A.M.	Lunch with Rotary Club.

	2:00 P.M.	Meet with maintenance to discuss faulty light fixture.
Wednesday	10:00 A.M.	Meet with Lorna, the payroll clerk, to discuss her appeal of her last performance appraisal.
	2:00 P.M.	Meet with all employees to discuss agenda items for Friday's departmental meeting.
Thursday	10:00 A.M.	Meet with accounting clerks to discuss problems they are experiencing with their immediate supervisor.
	2:00 P.M.	Meet with accounts receivable supervisor to discuss slow learning by new clerk, despite the new 300-page detailed manual.
Friday	9:00 A.M.	Meet with my supervisor to discuss apparent discrepancies in last month's reports.
	3:00 P.M.	Staff meeting with all accounting people, in order to come up with good ideas on how to improve effectiveness and efficiency. [John had passed out a copy of *In Search of Excellence* to the accounting area. It was disappointing that no one ever came up with a good idea—and these meetings usually lasted just 15 minutes or so, with John doing all the talking.]

PROJECTS/REPORTS

Between all of the telephone calls, meetings, and interruptions, John was supposed to be writing reports on:

1. Getting next year's budget in on time to director's office.
2. Slow response time of the computer network on the fifth floor, which was a frustrating problem for the clerks who used networked microcomputers. The problem was likely to worsen with the increasing workload.
3. Analysis of the "memo war" between John and the training unit over expense claims (the deputy director had been drawn in to arbitrate).

PROCRASTINATION

With all of the day-to-day things going on, John was having a difficult time keeping up; he was beginning to feel very stressed and was putting off reading his E-mail messages and writing the expected daily short memos, as well as not working on the major reports.

John wasn't too worried, however. He had always come through in the "crunch" before. In fact, John seems to like the adrenaline rush when faced with deadlines, even back to his days in high school.

PLANNING AHEAD

In the past, John worked all night and/or over a weekend to get caught up. Now, however, that option was not as available. He was getting a little older and could no longer stay alert during extended marathons. More importantly, perhaps, his wife, Mary, was taking weekend courses at the university to complete her Bachelor of Nursing degree and he was responsible for watching the children.

It was now 6:00 P.M. John was a half-hour later than he had told Mary. He did have a better overview of the day-to-day problems, but nothing was resolved on the better use of his time.

∽∘∾
INSTRUCTIONS AND QUESTIONS

1. What steps could John take to deal more effectively with the different sources of stress he encounters (phone calls, social interruptions, meetings, business reports, and so forth)?
2. Keep a log of your own activities for one week. What are your biggest "time wasters"? How can you manage your time more effectively?

PART THREE

Organizational and Leadership Issues

		Page
16.	Agency Capture?	89
17.	Delilah's In-Basket	90
18.	Dilemma in Juvenile Court	96
19.	Effective Leadership?	104
20.	Going to the Dogs!	106
21.	Hail to the New Chief	109
22.	Shifting the Costs of Governance	112

16

Agency Capture?

The State of Everywhere's Department of Forestry is undergoing some major challenges. The department has been around 40 years and, from the very beginning, it has had a very close relationship with its strongest clientele—the timber industry—especially the Everywhere Timber Producers Association (ETPA), the group of large timber companies in the state. It also has a small secondary clientele in the Everywhere Hunters Association.

In addition, the Department of Forestry has a very strong working relationship with the Everywhere House and Senate Committees on Agriculture, especially the subcommittees on forestry development.

However, in the last five years a major challenge has developed from the environmental movement, especially the Coalition for Everywhere's Forests (CEF). They played a minor role in the election of the new governor. His appointment of Mike Cleary as Director of the Forest Department was also the choice of the ETPA. Mike is a realist, however, and is concerned that the department must be more responsive to broader "citizen" interests, especially the CEF.

∽∘∽
INSTRUCTIONS AND QUESTIONS

You are Mr. Cleary's new executive assistant. In a two-page memo, outline to Mr. Cleary the agency's "dilemma" and ways to expand the department's base of support, given the real problems of "capture." But remember, the Director has his job partially because of the timber producers.

17

Delilah's In-Basket

Congratulations, Delilah Green. You have just been appointed Assistant Chief Engineer in charge of the Planning Branch of the Mid-State Transit Authority. It is the first day in your new assignment, and as a newcomer to the Authority, you feel both excited and anxious. You have come in early to review the briefing materials prepared for you by the Branch Administrative Assistant, who will be your primary staff person.

A number of issues are covered in the materials. As the chief planner, you have a broad range of responsibilities. But you are drawn to one package of materials marked with a big, red "expedite" tag. It includes the following 14 items:

1. An E-mail message from your new boss Bob Baxter, Deputy Chief Engineer in charge of the Facilities Division.
   The message advises you that you have a problem with the management of the Environmental Planning Section (EPS) of your branch. He indicates that this is a high priority and that the way you handle this problem may be a big factor in determining whether or not you pass your probationary period in your new position.

2. A synopsis of the history of EPS.
   For decades, the Mid-State Transit Authority has constructed, maintained, and operated an integrated transportation system. About four years ago, in response to state and federal legislation, the agency created an Environmental Planning Section, or EPS. This was a new function for the old-line engineering organization, which

had paid little attention to environmental impact during most of its history.

EPS was quickly staffed with a variety of highly qualified science and social science professionals from outside the Authority, and with several mid-level administrators who were reassigned from other branches. The professionals' jobs are to perform the studies in the various specialties. The administrators' jobs are to contract for consultant services, process invoices for payment, and do technical writing and editing of environmental impact statements.

There has been a great deal of turmoil and turnover in the managerial ranks of the agency during the period since the section was established. A rapid turnover of managers at the branch and division levels created such confusion that, for the first two years of operation, the section manager position was allowed to remain vacant. Nominally, the section was supervised by the Assistant Chief Engineer or by the Deputy Chief Engineer directly. In fact, much of the time the section was allowed to go its own way without supervision. For the past two years the EPS manager has been John Samson.

3. An organization chart showing the relationships of the various divisions, branches, sections, and units of the authority. (See Exhibit 17-1.)

4. Copies of memos and E-mail messages dating back over a year, signed by Mr. Baxter, which indicate that there have been a number of poor work products and missed deadlines from EPS.

5. A personnel roster showing that all EPS employees have permanent civil-service status in their present grades.

6. Copies of E-mail messages and memos from John Samson to various members of the EPS staff, documenting failure to perform assigned tasks in a satisfactory manner.

7. Copies of E-mail messages and memos with responses from staff members stating that they did their work well, that the problem is with the section manager, who they feel is incompetent, and that they were better off before he came, when they ran things by committee.

8. A fax from a consultant, complaining that he had not been paid for over six months.

9. Copies of Samson's performance reports indicating an increasing level of competence as a manager over a one-year probationary period. The final report rates all categories as outstanding. The reports were prepared by your predecessor and were all countersigned by Mr. Baxter.

Exhibit 17-1.

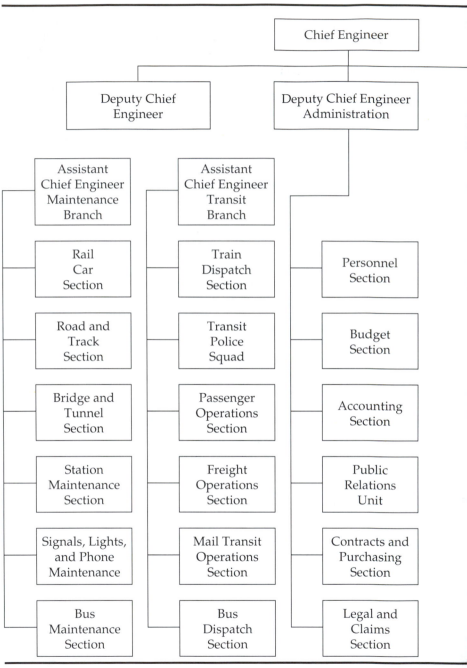

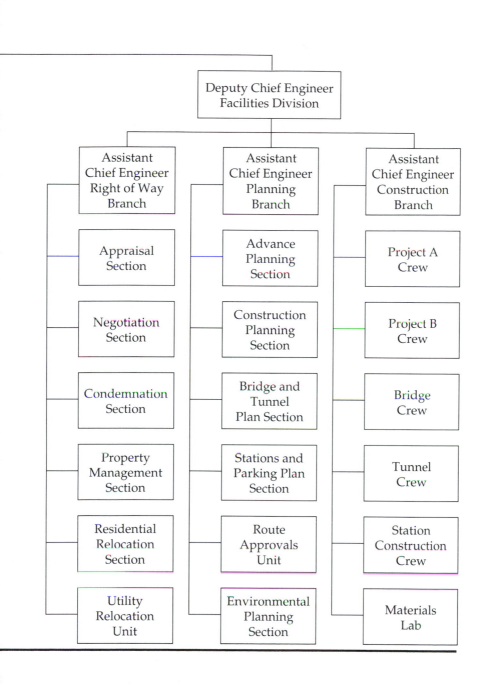

10. An E-mail message from the chief of a section located adjacent to the conference room, complaining that during the last EPS staff meeting the yelling was so loud that his staff could not concentrate on their work.
11. A budget printout indicating that the EPS is expending its travel budget at twice the rate authorized and that the money will be all gone by mid-year.
12. A petition from seven of the fourteen section staff members requesting that Mr. Samson be removed as section manager.
13. An E-mail from John Samson, requesting to meet with you regarding certain disciplinary actions that he wants you to take in regard to certain members of his staff. The E-mail states that Samson feels he has never had adequate support from above and that he hopes you will provide that support.
14. A memo from the Branch Administrative Assistant, written informally in his own handwriting, in response to a phone call you made to him last week. It reads, in part:

> …I don't know if the situation in EPS can be saved. Several of the staff members have been around a long time, and their "old boy" network extends clear to the Chief Engineer's staff. They have Samson buffaloed; they know it, and they love it. I have heard that they boast openly that they are going to get him.
>
> …John clearly doesn't have control at this point. His efforts are mostly concentrated on dealing with the hard-core group and on personally getting the work done that they don't. The rest of the staff gets very little supervision.… It may not be John's fault entirely that the situation has progressed to this point. This is his first management position and he has had precious little guidance from above. But he has contributed to it by not taking action to gain control of the unit.
>
> …By the way, Bob [Baxter] has been waiting for you to come on board to solve this problem. Informally, he has told me that he thinks you should fire John. But let me warn you that it takes at least four months to fill a position due to the delays in processing paperwork in the system. Incidently, three of the four people who can be reached on the civil service list for section manager are contract administrators in EPS and are part of the group that is giving John such a bad time.
>
> …One last thing: I think that this situation is affecting John's health. He hasn't looked well for some time and his use of sick leave is way up. As a friend, I asked him once why he doesn't just demote back to his previous position. But he has a kid in college and is just a few years away from retirement. He feels that he can't afford to take the cut in salary.

After reviewing this material you realize that you have about one-half hour left before the working day begins. Soon Mr. Baxter, Samson, and the entire planning staff will start drifting into the office. You have no doubt in your mind that several of the parties to the EPS problem will be wanting to know what you are going to do. You decide to take the time you have left to determine an immediate course of action, and to begin planning the steps you will take to achieve a long-term solution.

∽०∾
INSTRUCTIONS AND QUESTIONS

You are Delilah. Review the 14 items and assign them priorities. Which are the most important and should get your attention first?

Now review your priorities. Why did you make the choices you did? Do you recognize some logic or theory underlying them?

You may gain perspective on your underlying logic or theory by discussing your priorities with other class members. Does their logic or theory differ from yours? Now choose some specific goals or objectives that you would like to characterize your leadership, if you did not do so before.

Do your priorities change?

18

Dilemma in Juvenile Court

The people of Tidewater County take pride in the fact that their county has ranked very high nationally in population growth for the past 20 years. Over the last three decades, the county has grown approximately eightfold.

The Juvenile Court of Tidewater reflects this growth. Initially the juvenile section was merely a branch of the Tidewater County Criminal Court. It then consisted of one counselor, Ellen Mann, who was responsible for all juvenile cases that were not handled informally by parents or small town police officers. In the last decade, state statutes set up a system of separate juvenile courts. A judge was elected in Tidewater, and Mann was made his sole assistant. Four years later, Mann hired Harry Barnes to assist her in processing the increasing number of juvenile referrals. The court grew steadily with the county and currently employs 20 counselors (see Exhibit 18-1).

Bill Jones comes to work for the court as a counselor after obtaining his degree in criminology and corrections in 1982 at the state university. He is appalled at the backward operation at Tidewater, one of the larger juvenile courts in the state. He finds that almost all other counselors share his evaluation, and he soon becomes their spokesperson. After much griping and complaining among the younger counselors, Jones drafts a recommendation and takes it directly to the judge (see Exhibit 18-2). Jones and his contemporaries are convinced that if the recommendation is adopted, the efficiency of the court will improve markedly.

Judge Smith is shaken when he reads the recommendation in Exhibit 18-2. He is surprised that Jones had brazenly brought the information

Exhibit 18-1.   Present Organization of Tidewater County
Juvenile Court

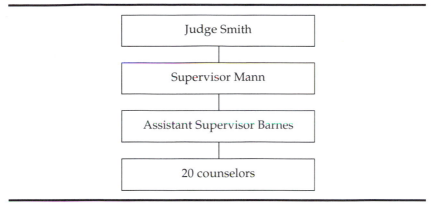

Judge Smith

Supervisor Mann

Assistant Supervisor Barnes

20 counselors

directly to him instead of sending it up through Barnes and then Mann, as the structure in Exhibit 18-1 provides.

Judge Smith feels a lot of questions need answers. Is it true that all the new counselors are as upset as Jones claims? Why hadn't someone told the judge that his employees are so unhappy? It seems as if he is always the last to know. If this situation should leak to the press, he might have problems in next year's election. The judge is a lawyer, not a social scientist or an administrator. What had Mann or Barnes been doing to rile up these youngsters so much?

Exhibit 18-3, showing how Jones thought the court was currently running, looks accurate enough. The judge does not get involved in the process until the counselor handling the case brings him the pretrial investigation and discusses it with him. This usually occurs just prior to the hearing. The judge is a little surprised at how complex Jones had made the process seem, but it does appear to be completely accurate.

It appears to the judge that Jones was right in his statement that it will not cost much to institute the proposed change. Moving a few desks and throwing up a few wall partitions in the main office building should do it.

Jones's approach is brash, but his plan does appear to have some merit. If the kid went singing to the press, Smith also muses, he could stir up a lot more trouble than he is worth.

Judge Smith is leaning toward trying the plan but decides to get Mann's view on it before making his move. "Ellen," the judge requests,

Exhibit 18-2. Recommendations from Counselors

Dear Judge Smith:

Your court is unhappy. The procedures followed here were outdated 20 years ago. All of the younger counselors agree with me; vast changes are needed.

The change that is needed most drastically, and could be instituted at very little cost, is a simple reorganization. The current counselor system stinks. As nearly as I can tell from observing it for a year, it works (or is supposed to work!) as I have depicted in the attached chart [see Exhibit 18-3]. The counties around us gave up this system some time ago. It simply places too much work on individual counselors. When counselors have to fool around with the police departments and running down parents for the first time, they let their probation work slip. If counselors concentrate on probation work (as they should!), the incoming cases stack up. This system would be fine if we only had three or four cases each to worry about. My current case load is 47 and growing every day.

I propose the system shown in the next two charts [see Exhibits 18-4 and 5]. This new system provides for a better division of work, specialization of counselors, and a more favorable span of control for the supervisors.

Respectfully yours,

Bill Jones

"I want you to take a look at this recommendation Jones handed me. I think the lad makes some good points, but I want your opinion before I make my decision."

Ellen Mann has her own questions as she scans Jones's recommendation. Why is Jones concerned about "flows" when he has so many cases that demand his time? Why hadn't Jones brought this thing to her in the first place instead of bothering the judge with it? Didn't Jones know that Mann was the supervisor?

Exhibit 18-3.   Present Flow of Cases

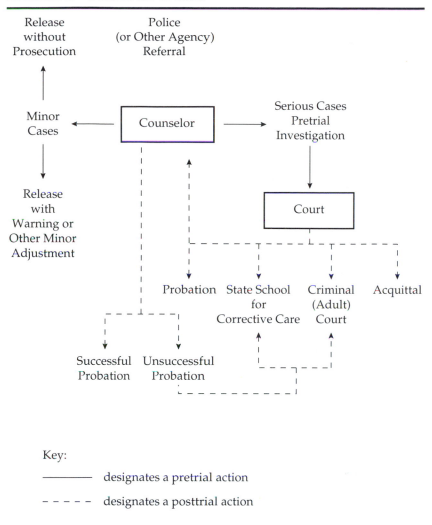

Key:

——————   designates a pretrial action

– – – – –   designates a posttrial action

Mann is certain about two things. First, she knows for a fact that the new counselors are unhappy. The Supreme Court has really messed up the works. Imagine, juveniles now have all the same rights as adults. That isn't right. The delinquents are all getting lawyers and beating the charges against them. Mann has seen the discontent grow among the newer counselors.

Exhibit 18-4.   Proposed Flow of Cases

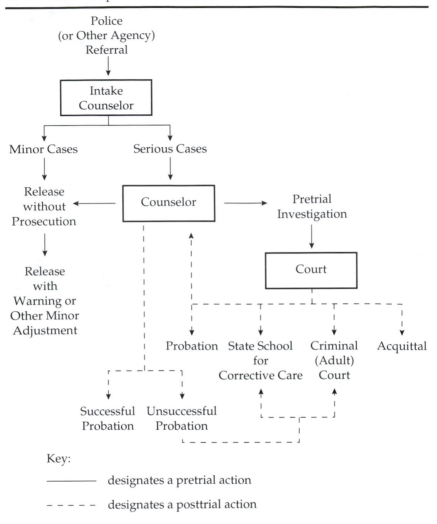

Key:

——————   designates a pretrial action

- - - - -   designates a posttrial action

Second, there is no way Mann's schedule and work habits will allow her to make any reasonable sense of Jones's proposal. She calls on her assistant, Barnes. "This gobbledygook gets worse every year, Harry," she says. "Decipher it, and give me a reading on it in the morning, will you?"

Barnes cannot believe what he reads. The kid has gone and done it. He has submitted an asinine proposal to Judge Smith. Barnes wonders

Exhibit 18-5.   Proposed Organization of Tidewater County Juvenile Court

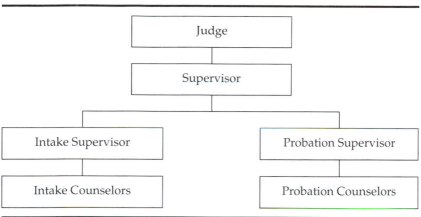

why he had not advised Mann against hiring that smart aleck a year ago. As assistant supervisor, it would have been easy for Barnes to convince Mann not to hire Jones in the first place.

Things had been smooth before Jones started as a counselor, Barnes fumes. Until Jones arrived, there were no radical troublemakers stirring up animosity in the court. The court functioned perfectly well for the 15 years Barnes worked for it. The old system functioned well with two employees, and it was functioning well with 20 counselors. Time had proven its effectiveness. Under this old system, each child referred to the court has a single counselor appointed, depending on the district in the county where the child resides. This one counselor receives the referral from the police, conducts the pretrial investigation (when necessary), and is the child's probation officer if the judge decides on probation.

The beauty of this system is its simplicity, Barnes believes. The same counselor works with the same child from the time of first report to the court until release from probation or confinement. Every counselor has the opportunity to really get to know each child assigned to him or her.

As a former counselor, Barnes does know what a headache the "intake" process is. The police report is usually full of errors. The court records have to be screened to see if the child has ever been before the court. The child's school performance also has to be reviewed. Moreover, letters have to be prepared requesting the parents to bring the child in for an initial interview. Finally, the parents have to be hunted down if they don't show. No doubt, intake processing is the worst job in the court.

But Barnes knows it can be done. In fact, he is the best intake counselor the court has. He knows the police and school officials, and he knows how to get parents and their children in for initial interviews.

Despite his competence with it, however, Barnes hates the intake process. He hates to have to run all over the county. He does not like to drive, and he does not like being out in the weather. As assistant supervisor, he is able to supervise the secretaries, run the office from inside, check the progress of cases, keep the court docket flowing, and devote a great deal of attention to his favorite area, probation counseling. Barnes is not about to casually threaten this personally comfortable situation.

In any case, Barnes considers the main goal of the court to be straightening out youngsters through probation. The probationers come in twice a month, report their grades and difficulties to the probation counselor, and are on their way. The counselor will make a little note as to what was said, and this will be entered into the child's file. The same counselor processes the intake, trial, and probation phases of each case. What could be more logical?

True enough, the adjacent counties had split their juvenile courts into intake and probation sections in the way Jones recommended. Any fool could see, though, that the rash reorganizations clearly had a disastrous effect on the morale of the personnel who were made intake counselors. Faced with the deluge of all the referrals in their respective counties, the relatively few intake counselors were unable to keep up.

Four of them in other counties left to go to other courts or agencies. It appeared strange to Barnes that, in spite of this, the governor's blue ribbon Committee on Juvenile Delinquency praised the action of these adjacent courts in adopting the newer system.

Barnes takes an early and definite position, as Jones learns when their paths accidentally cross as they are leaving the office on the very afternoon that the memo made the rounds. Jones had never seen Barnes so angry. The words are not merely spoken; Barnes spits them out at Jones. "So you thought things used to be miserable around here? Just wait...."

Several colleagues observe the encounter, and word gets quickly back to Judge Smith.

∽○∾

INSTRUCTIONS AND QUESTIONS

You are Judge Smith. You felt you might face a real dilemma when you received Jones's memo. Now you are certain of it.

1. Describe the dilemma as accurately as you can.
2. Can you see any ways of avoiding the horns of the dilemma? Your first thought is to make Jones the new intake supervisor and let him live with his recommendations. But you are fearful that Barnes will fight any change. Consider the proposal as an "organizational design" issue utilizing more contemporary theories. Now analyze the situation and proposal.

    What is the best course of action? Why?

19

Effective Leadership?

June has accepted the position of Records and Support Office Manager with a medium-size police department. The Records and Support Division is the information center for the entire police department. The civilian position pays considerably well and provides desirable working hours. The position requires the supervision of the Telephone Response, Data Entry, and Report Retrieval Units, which include a total of eight subordinates. These units require computer operation, as well as communication and filing skills. June reports directly to James Matthews, the Records and Support Captain, who then reports directly to the Police Chief, Stan Wilhite.

During the first few days of orientation and observation, June received information from several co-workers and subordinates regarding the previous manager, Bob Lacert, who retired with over 20 years of service time in the position. It was stated that he lacked interest in innovation and efficiency. It was also stated that he was deficient in the management skills needed to perform in the position adequately. After the first week as manager, June noticed that several of her subordinates appeared to lack motivation and effort. As a result of her observation, she reviewed the past performance appraisal scores of the subordinates. She found that the score of "average" had been used consistently by her predecessor for the entire staff. June also was unable to find any documentation regarding previous appraisal interviews. Contrary to the low motivation and effort, the employees appeared to have adequate training in completing the relatively simple and repetitive tasks.

June also noticed problems with the effectiveness of the units. The organization of the tasks appeared to be inefficient. This was evident by the number of lost incident reports and the inability to track documentation at any given time.

As a positive note, June found that her subordinates appeared to be team players and that signs of cohesion were visible.

Through further observations, she concluded that the three units were hampered by limited technology. For example, incident reports were being typed into the computer system and then individually filed.

She also found a lack of adequate support and assistance from other units within the department. Other units not located in the same building, such as Narcotics, Special Investigations, and the Southwest Precinct, transferred and retrieved information through the Records and Support Division. Limited structure in the information system appeared to cause external coordination problems. Untimely pickup and delivery of documentation was one of the visible dilemmas.

On Monday of her second week, June attended a departmental meeting in which an announcement was made by Stan Wilhite. He stated his immediate retirement intentions and the hiring of Larry Banks as his successor. The department officials did not seem to be shocked by the announcement. After adjournment of the meeting, June met with James in the hallway. He stated that the announcement of the Chief's retirement wasn't a surprise, but that the hiring of Larry Banks was. He further stated that Mr. Banks was recruited from the "large" San Diego Police Department and is known to be an innovator who strives to increase organizational efficiency.

∽०∾
INSTRUCTIONS AND QUESTIONS

1. How can June increase the motivation and effort of her subordinates?
2. Why wasn't Bob Lacert's leadership style particularly effective?
3. What strategies can June implement to create the efficiency that in all likelihood Larry Banks will require?

20

Going to the Dogs!

Covington County, Virginia, is a rural district about 50 miles south of Richmond which historically has been dominated by farms and small towns. But, as the Washington-Richmond corridor has become more populated, other residents and developments have moved into Covington. So far, the impact has been slight. Some federal employees and other professionals who work in the Washington-Richmond corridor have bought houses here and commute to their jobs. A few small industries have also bought parcels of rural acreage for future building sites.

One of the first signs of change in the life of Covington County is a newly enacted dog-licensing ordinance. Several of the new "suburban" residents in Covington were bothered by the numerous stray dogs that frequently wandered across their yards, frightening their children and soiling their grass. Historically, these country dogs simply roamed free, seldom bothering anyone. But now, at least according to the newer residents of Covington County, the dogs are a public nuisance.

As a consequence, the young professionals organized a campaign to pressure the County Commission to require that every dog in Covington have a $25 license. Pet owners were subject to a stiff fine if their animals were caught wandering about. The dog-licensing campaign—complete with charts showing the increasing dog population, reports detailing the health and safety hazards of stray dogs, and testimony from local residents about specific troublesome incidents with loose dogs—took the County Commission by storm. The County Commissioners were simply overwhelmed by such a well-organized and sophisticated political campaign. They immediately passed the new dog-license ordinance.

While passage of the dog-license ordinance was easy, its implementation proved to be more difficult. Older residents of Covington County saw no reason for the law and resented the $25 registration fee. A tide of resistance to the new license law developed and was soon organized and led by a senior local resident, Roderic Shortridge, Esquire.

Roderic Shortridge came from an old, prominent Covington County family noted for its conservative views. The Covington Shortridges believed that "their county" was the most beautiful and prosperous in all Virginia and should not change. Some older residents felt the Shortridge family still had never gotten over "the Disestablishment of the Anglican Church." And, Roderic Shortridge saw this new dog-license law as evidence of even more subversion of traditional values than that situation! A retired lawyer, who now bred foxhounds on his 200-acre farm of rolling green countryside, Roderic Shortridge had the knowledge, experience, and prestige to take on the new forces of change in Covington County. And he was going to start with that dog-license law!

Roderic Shortridge, Esquire, ran for a County Commission seat the following fall on a "Repeal the Dog License" platform. He traveled the county (usually with a few foxhounds in tow) preaching the gospel of "dog-rights and traditional rural virtue." He railed vehemently against the intrusion of "city elements" and their newfangled ideas. He reminded the good citizens of Covington County that foxhounds and beagles had been roaming free in Covington without licenses *before* Washington, D.C., was built—even before the American Revolution. All of this was pretty persuasive to the older residents of Covington County, and Roderic Shortridge was elected to the Commission by a large majority. He proceeded to effect what one liberal news commentator called "The Counter-Reformation in Covington County."

First, Commissioner Shortridge persuaded his fellow County Commissioners to repeal the dog-license law. Then, he got them to pass resolutions discouraging industrial development and suburban growth in Covington County. He went after the School Board and Corrections Department next for their liberal textbook and penal policies. As time went on, Covington County gained a reputation as a backward, reactionary region, which led commuter-residents to consider moving to more progressive and hospitable environments. Industrial development in Covington also began to drop off as corporate planners were called before the County Commission and given the third degree. All in all, Covington County was rapidly developing a reputation as an island of backwardness and poverty (with lower public services, poorer quality schools, and so forth) in a sea of development and prosperity spilling over from the Washington-Richmond corridor.

The newer residents of the county continued to try to develop the region with new businesses, restaurants, and industry, but they faced some stiff resistance, not only from Commissioner Shortridge and his "Old Guard," but also from some of the younger residents. The residents who shared Shortridge's values of a simple, rural existence without industrial pollution, government regulation, and shopping malls saw themselves as environmentalists simply protecting the quality of community life for themselves and their children. However, as time went on, enough Yuppies (Young Urban Professionals) moved into Covington County and became active politically. This group was able to get five new members (out of 10) elected on the County Commission and to persuade the Commission to hire a County Manager. The newer residents of Covington County were confident that a professional administrator would support their progressive views and control the conservative and environmentalist elements in county government. The war in Covington County may go on, but the newer residents felt they had won a decisive battle by getting a professional County Manager.

✿✿✿

INSTRUCTIONS AND QUESTIONS

Imagine that you are the new County Manager in Covington County.

1. How would you approach the various groups in Covington County politics and the county as a whole?
2. What policies might you fight for in the short term and in the long term?
3. What obstacles might you encounter with those policies?
4. What do you see for Covington County's future economic development?
4. Discuss the major leadership differences between a professional manager type of government and a purely elected local government.

21

Hail to the New Chief

Bill Pickles has been promoted to Regional Health Officer of the State Health Department, which provides a wide range of medical services to clientele not covered by general healthcare programs. As Regional Health Officer, Bill is in charge of almost 100 employees in a wide range of professions (e.g., nurse practitioners, psychologists, pharmacists, and lab technicians) that serve 10 counties.

During Bill's early efforts to become acquainted with his new job, he discovers that considerable fragmentation and conflict exist within the health department, and this is causing reduced efficiency in service delivery. The department is made up of people from the local area (primarily staff and administrative personnel, but some technicians also) and people recruited from around the nation (primarily doctors, pharmacists, and other professionals from large universities).

Some tension seems to exist between the two groups, as well as a split between older and younger employees of the agency. The older personnel tend to see the department as relying more on local businesses for supplies and service, while the younger employees urge bringing in the most advanced technology from national and international companies. In addition to these conflicts, there is considerable tension between sections in the department. The technicians and lab workers think that the administrative personnel are foolish and "unscientific." The administrators and staff personnel think the technicians are narrow-minded, overly specialized, and ignorant of political realities. One of the older administrators is fond of saying: "There's no room for pure science in public service."

These various conflicts in the department seem to have been exacerbated by Bill's predecessor. Bill learns that the former Regional Health Officer had been ineffectual in dealing with departmental problems and shied away from making decisions. He had been brought in from another state with an impressive record in public health administration, but he quickly alienated many in the department by reorganizing the sections to give more power to his newly appointed staff. He further upset some members of the department by hiring his mother-in-law as an "Executive Assistant to the Regional Health Officer" at a salary higher than most professionals in the department. When employees came to him with problems or complaints, he seemed alternately uninterested or unsympathetic. Occasionally he feigned interest by saying, "I'll take care of that right away," and then never did anything at all. Health Department personnel noticed that this Regional Health Officer was primarily interested in remodeling his home. Whenever a lapse in the conversation occurred, he would start talking about various projects he had undertaken.

Bill realizes that many of the conflicts in the department are due to the inept leadership of his predecessor, but visits from his employees during the first few months of his new position also reveal deeper problems. The first visitor is an elderly member of the staff (Bill Hicks) who grew up in the area and joined the department at 20 years of age. He says:

> This here department was much nicer when it was smaller. Back in the old days we were like a family here. We took care of everyone in this area and didn't work too hard. I know I speak for many here when I say that this department was better back then. All these young whippersnappers from the city with fancy degrees from Harvard and the University of Kentucky, they've ruined this department. We oughta get rid of 'em and make this place like it usta be.

Bill's next visitor is a young pharmacist who came from Boston to work for the health department two years ago. He says:

> Hi there! My name is James Youngblood. I can't tell you how glad I am to see a new Regional Health Officer here. That old guy, what a jerk! Can you believe it? All he could talk about was remodeling his house! But now we've got a new, dynamic leader and things are really going to take off! I've written down a few ideas for you to consider (he hands you a 350-page typed manuscript) for improving the department. The first thing is to get rid of all those old fogies! What a lot of deadwool we have floating around here! We've got to transfer all of our contracts to IBM and get the latest computers! It's really going to be exciting!

Several other members of the department visit Bill with additional problems, and he asks them about his earlier visitors. Most think Bill Hicks is a nice old fellow, but point out that he has frequent lapses of memory and often is found sleeping under his desk. James Youngblood is considered very talented and dynamic, but he has had affairs with every secretary in the department.

As Bill considers the problem inside his department, two crises occur. First, a memo comes from the State Health Director, saying that the State General Assembly is threatening to cut the Health Department's budget, beginning with the least efficient Regional Offices (such as his). Second, Bill arrives at work the next day to find every secretary (except the former Regional Health Officer's mother-in-law) marching in a picket line protesting for higher wages and a union. All of the other employees (except James Youngblood) are hanging out the windows watching the secretaries march. This strike further cripples the department, just when the State General Assembly is looking for places to cut the budget.

∽०∾

INSTRUCTIONS AND QUESTIONS

1. Discuss the major problems at this department.
2. Imagine you are Bill Pickles. How would you handle the immediate crises and how would you improve the organization in the long term?

22

Shifting the Costs of Governance

PART ONE

Western State is large in area and small in population. Much of the state consists of grasslands and forest, and most of the population is concentrated in a single major urban area and in a few smaller cities, one of which is the state capital. The economy of Western State has been battered by high interest rates and recession in the past two years, and things are not looking brighter for the current year. Furthermore, the state legislature is vigorously responding to nationwide taxpayer discontent with proposed tax reductions and expenditure controls. The combination of economic and political conditions has sent state employees scurrying for ways to cut costs—often in unexpected ways

As an analyst for the Legislative Counsel's Office, you know this only too well. In your capacity as a member of the budgetary committee's staff you not only undertake your own searches for economies, but also review proposals from the many agencies you examine. You know that there are few simple answers. Every change turns out to have ramifications previously unrecognized.

Take the medical examiner, for instance. No one really knows why the medical examiner's office was set up as it is. Several important people do know that the current organization and method of financing ought to be changed. However, how the new organization and financing plan should be designed is still a mystery. Consequently, determining that design is your "mission impossible."

Currently the medical examiner is a state employee, with three professional assistants and an appropriation of $846,201, according to the state's biennial budget. The major portion of the funds, $431,623, is for personal services, not including clerical assistance. The office operates under the administrative control of the State Department of Health, and the medical examiner is a medical doctor, board certified in pathology and with additional certification and special residencies in forensic medicine. The medical examiner and two professional assistants have their office in Metropolitan County, the state's major urban area and the location of its largest city. The fourth pathologist is located in the second largest metropolitan area. In addition, the examiner and the three assistants travel throughout the state as required.

According to law, the medical examiner's office provides medical examining services for both routine and unusual cases in Metropolitan County. The office also maintains its laboratory there. The county does not have any other medical examining service. The state pays 100 percent of the costs of the medical examining services for Metropolitan County and 50 percent of the costs in the next largest county. That county maintains its own medical examiner, in addition.

In the rest of the state, including the capital, there are no full-time medical examiners. Routine cases are handled by local physicians appointed to act as medical examiner. But physicians without special training and facilities are not able to handle unusual causes of death, decomposed bodies, and other infrequent problems. The state medical examiner handles these cases, either directly or by providing technical assistance and laboratory services, and provides the court testimony if necessary. The law stipulates that the state can pay up to 50 percent of the costs of medical examining in these areas not otherwise covered by statute. In recent years, the legislature has eliminated this appropriation—approximately $90,500—and in the current biennium the state is paying for virtually no services outside Metropolitan County and the next largest county. The less urban counties have been upset by this change, as they, too, have felt the effects of fiscal strain. However, they benefit from formal training conducted throughout the state, and continue to receive direct assistance for difficult cases, consultation, lab services, and case review. Case reviews and consultations totaled 16,826 over the last two yearly fiscal periods. Direct state autopsies totaled 1,274, with reimbursed autopsies projected at 700. Training for both police and court officials as well as for acting medical examiners reaches approximately 800 persons throughout the state. Lab services total 2,700 individual billings. All funds available are state general funds.

∽o∾
INSTRUCTIONS AND QUESTIONS

1. Analyze the current arrangement for the medical examiner. List its strengths and weaknesses and identify who benefits from or is disadvantaged by each.
2. Once you have completed your list, outline a preferable arrangement. Pay attention to financing, equity, workload, and third-party interest, as well as to immediate institutional concerns and principles of organization.

PART TWO

The Department of Health hints that it will not put up a strong fight to maintain its control over the medical examiner's office. You begin to search for a new organizational location. One of your legislators proposes making the function a local responsibility and getting the state out of it entirely. The medical examiner replies that this would leave the rural areas unable to service unusual cases since, in the absence of a state office, there would no longer be a central laboratory and technical assistance function.

A second suggestion is to maintain the state medical examiner's office, but to bill the counties for the service. Metropolitan County legislators do not support this part of the previous proposal. Rural legislators also demur, feeling that both of these proposals are likely to leave rural areas paying more than their fair share of the costs.

∽o∾
INSTRUCTIONS AND QUESTIONS

1. Analyze these two proposals in two ways. First look at them in businesslike terms—fixed and variable costs, routine and nonroutine services, economies of scale, possibilities for various service contracting agreements, and the like.
2. Next, analyze these proposals in more political and governmental terms, including how necessary services can be assured, who pays for the services and whether the costs are shared equitably, what political claims are likely to be made regarding alternative uses for the money spent for medical examining, what the proper division of responsibility is between state and local government, who specifically gets the business if the state gives it up, and the like.

PART THREE

Western State recently passed a reorganization of the trial court system. Costs in the trial court system had been growing between 20 and 25 percent per year for almost a decade. The trial courts during this period were agencies of county government. The Association of County Governments had fought for several years for the state to assume responsibility for the trial courts. Finally, in the most recent biennium, the legislature agreed to assume this responsibility. The legislature agreed, however, only with the provision that state financing of the trial courts would be phased in gradually during the current and following biennia, with full state financing coming in five years. At the same time, the reorganization bill included hefty increases in all court-related fees to provide revenue for this new state responsibility.

The prosecutors remain county employees with some state financial assistance, especially for complex, expensive, or widely publicized cases. The state continues, as before, to provide the majority of the financing for indigent defense.

∽o∾

INSTRUCTIONS AND QUESTIONS

In a draft memorandum to the Legislative Counsel, outline the pros and cons of placing the medical examiner's office with the trial courts. Summarize in your memo your analyses from the previous two parts of the case.

PART FOUR

Organizational Change and Culture

		Page
23.	A License for Quality: TQM at the BMV	119
24.	Doing Hard Time: Reforming the Prison System	125
25.	Environmental Quality	128
26.	Mixed Effects of a Demonstration Project	129

23

A License for Quality: TQM at the BMV

INTRODUCTION

Total Quality Management (TQM)* is a controversial management technique now popular in business and industry. TQM's success has forced managers to examine possible applications in public agencies. Concurrently, TQM has failed in some organizations and has many detractors. With this in mind, a brief introduction to TQM follows.

WHAT IS TQM?

TQM is really not new. Rather is represents a return to "good" management practices. Instead of focusing on outputs (and detecting errors after they have occurred), the emphasis is on the process of producing the service. A key element in TQM is to identify the customer (client) and the "suppliers," both external and internal to the agency. A customer uses the services of the agency; internal customers might include staff or units and divisions that rely on others within the agency for services. Thus, a computer unit might supply other offices with services and might also deal directly with external customers. Suppliers, on

---

*For the purposes of this case, "Total Quality Management" is used interchangeably with "Continuous Improvement Process" (CIP). In public, educational, and not-for-profit organizations, CIP may be a preferable term.

the other hand, provide the materials necessary for the job. An internal supplier might be the purchasing office that buys paper in bulk and distributes it within the agency. On the other hand, external suppliers are outside vendors who supply materials and resources to the organization.

TQM is comprised of two components: data and group process. Both components are necessary for successful implementation and each has specific tools that work groups may use (see appendix to this case). The following outline of *"How to TQM"* shows the interrelationship between these two components.

Starting at the beginning: Who are "we"? An important precursor to the use of TQM is to identify the key players. TQM begins with a project or projects at the unit level and chosen by the employees in that work group. As a first step, the group reviews their mission (or goals) and identifies both internal and external customers and suppliers.

HOW TO TQM

- **Identifying the Process to Be Improved.** To be effective, work unit members should identify the process to improve (to "TQM"). Brainstorming and nominal group technique (see appendix for brief description of tools) help the group identify and agree upon the process.
- **Gathering Data.** Once the work unit has chosen a process to improve, members study the process and may employ some of these techniques for gathering data: flow charts, check sheets, histograms, and fishbone diagrams. It is important for the work unit to observe the process and to ask suppliers and customers for feedback on their perceptions of the process.
- **Taking Action.** Once the process is documented, the work group discusses problems and maps ways in which the process can be improved. The nominal group technique might be used again to help the group reach consensus on the action to take.
- **Checking the Results.** Once changes are implemented, data should be gathered again so that the process can be studied and improved. This continual attention to improvement is an important part of TQM.

THE CASE

You have just been appointed director of the Bureau of Motor Vehicles (BMV) office in a suburban location in a large southern state. Your selection coincides with a purge in the agency following a scandal involving the selling of driver's licenses to illegal aliens, irregularities in license plate renewals, and continuing criticism of the agency's services from the media, taxpayers, legislators, and the governor. Your location is in the suburbs of the capital city and is the test site for system changes. You have a free hand to make changes, but can expect close scrutiny from the director, governor, legislature, and media. You decide to initiate a TQM program as a means of improving quality and effecting change.

You meet with managers and employees, and they decide to focus on two areas: driver's license applications/renewals and license plate renewals. You have been given permission to experiment with pricing, including accepting credit cards for services (entailing a 12 percent bank service fee), giving discounts to encourage better utilization of services, surcharges for premium services, and extended hours and flexible scheduling for employees (normal working hours are 8:00 A.M.–4:30 P.M.). You should assume that the public employee union is willing to cooperate for this TQM "experiment"; however, the union expects employees to be rewarded for any productivity gains or cost savings. Assume that no changes will require legislative approval.

DRIVER'S LICENSE APPLICATIONS AND RENEWALS

New license applicants and renewal applicants report to separate but adjacent desks in the office. When the office is busy, consumers often stand in the wrong line and discover their mistake only after a long wait. In an effort to identify failing eyesight in older drivers, all applicants must take an eye test, so all lines merge at the "Eye Zone." After the eye test, first-time drivers or those with expired licenses must wait in line for a driving test.

All applicants pay the driver's license fee at the next desk, cash only. All first-time drivers and all applicants with out-of-state licenses must take the written test. First-time drivers must pass both the driving and written portions of the test on the same day; otherwise, both tests must be retaken.

A clerk checks the computer for any outstanding ticket or arrest warrants against the applicants. Finally, all applicants fill out an application form, the data are entered into the computer, a picture is taken, and a driver's license is made. Organ donor stickers are available in a box by the door.

The most popular times for renewals are 11:00 A.M.–4:00 P.M. Because of the large number of younger, first-time applicants, most of these occur after 2:00 P.M. The flow is lightest before 11:30 A.M. on Mondays, Tuesdays, and Wednesdays.

LICENSE PLATE RENEWALS

All license plates must be renewed in person; if a vehicle is jointly titled, either both owners must come into the office together, or the "absent" owner must complete a power of attorney form, which is available in the office. In the case of retitling after death of one of the co-owners, both a death certificate and court order are required to change the plates.

All license plates expire on January 31 of every year. Approximately 80 percent of the renewals are done between Thanksgiving and the deadline; 60 percent are done in the last month; 35 percent are done in the last week of January; and 3 percent are done after the deadline. The lines at all BMV offices in the state extend into the street during the last two weeks in January; this attracted added media attention when one applicant had a heart attack after waiting in line for three hours in 30-degree weather last year.

The regular staff can handle 40 renewals per hour, except during the lunch hour, when only half that number can be processed. During the month of January, temporary workers are hired, but due to their inexperience, the same number of temporary employees as the regular staff can process only 25 renewals per hour. Once inside the office, the single queue divides into several lines; sometimes it is difficult to cut lines off when workers need to take breaks.

The documents required for the renewal are the title, original proof of insurance, and the annual vehicle inspection certificate. Only cash is accepted, and only certain employees are bonded to handle cash, so the last step in the process is the "cash desk." It is September 1, and you want to implement changes by November 1.

∽o∾
INSTRUCTIONS AND QUESTIONS

For this case, evaluate:

1. What is the mission?
2. Who are the internal and external customers?
3. Who are the internal and external suppliers?
4. What is the process for driver's license applications and renewals? For license plate renewals? (Develop a flowchart of the existing process.)

5. How can the processes be redesigned? (Develop a flowchart for the "re-designed" processes.)
6. What are the problems in implementing the changes?
7. What are some "unintended" consequences of the changes you proposed?

Appendix: TQM Tools

BRAINSTORMING

a) *What?*   Tool to use in generating ideas.
b) *When?*   Use in group setting to generate ideas; maximizes creativity of group. May be first step in using another tool (such as fishbone diagram).
c) *How?*   Select recorder; generate ideas (no evaluation); record ideas; ask for clarification.

FLOWCHART

a) *What?*   A picture of any process (events, steps, activities, tasks).
b) *When?*   Use if a visual representation of the process is needed. Try to see the "big picture," including the relationships between people and tasks.
c) *How?*   Observe the process; identify the players; list the steps in the process; draw the representation of the steps/players.

NOMINAL GROUP TECHNIQUE (NGT)

a) *What?*   Structured group process to help make a decision.
b) *When?*   Use when you want every group member to take part in the decision. It can be used when one or two people are dominating the group.
c) *How?*   Presentation of question; development of master list; master list clarification; initial ranking of items; discussion; final listing of items by group.

CHECK SHEET

a) *What?*   Tool for collecting data in consistent form. Most commonly, check sheet is a tally arranged in columns or matrices.
b) *When?*   Use to collect data; especially useful when several people are gathering data.
c) *How?*   List data needs; decide on form; design and produce check sheet; gather and report data.

SCATTER DIAGRAM

a) *What?*   Statistical tool visually shows the relationship between two variables, if one exists.
b) *When?*   Use when you want to determine the relationship of one variable to another.
c) *How?*   Gather data; draw vertical and horizontal axes; plot data; interpret.

HISTOGRAM

a) *What?*   Statistical tool; a bar graph of data.
b) *When?*   Use to examine set of related variables.
c) *How?*   Gather data; select groups ("classes"); draw vertical and horizontal axes; plot data; interpret.

FISHBONE (CAUSE & EFFECT) DIAGRAM

a) *What?*   Picture of various elements of a system that may contribute to a problem.
b) *When?*   Use to identify root cause of problem when there are differing opinions on the cause.
c) *How?*   Identify problem; record problem statement; draw fishbone; brainstorm causes; identify most likely cause (can use nominal group process). As a second step, you may repeat the diagramming process for the root cause.

24

Doing Hard Time: Reforming the Prison System

Bolman and Deal* identify four viewpoints or frames for use in studying people and organizations: *structural, human resources, political,* and *symbolic.* The "structural frame,"[†] based in the field of sociology, emphasizes the structure of an organization, and focuses on rules, procedures, roles, relationships, policies, and hierarchies. By contrast, the "human resource frame" is grounded in organizational psychology and focuses on the fit between the individual and the organization. Individuals' goals, needs, and feelings, and how to fulfill them are paramount. The "political frame," developed by political scientists, considers organizations as screaming jungles in which individuals and groups jockey for scarce resources and power. Key activities of this frame include bargaining, negotiation, and compromise. Finally, the "symbolic frame" uses social and cultural anthropology to examine organizations, putting aside all assumptions of linearity and rationality—the meaning of what happened rather than the what is important. This frame views organizations as tribes, theater, or carnivals. Organizations are "cultures"[‡] peopled by heroes and propelled by myths, stories, fairy tales, rituals, and ceremonies.

While the political actions drive much of what goes on at higher levels in public agencies, the symbolic frame affords opportunities for

*Bolman, Lee G., and Terrence E. Deal. 1991. *Reframing Organizations: Artistry, Choice and Leadership.* San Francisco: Jossey-Bass.

[†]The frame descriptions are drawn from Bolman and Deal (1991), pp. 15–16.

[‡]This perspective is commonly termed "organizational culture."

public managers to accomplish change. This frame is particularly appropriate in settings with conflicting or unclear goals, multiple constituencies, uncertainty, or calls for reform. According to Bolman and Deal, the *symbolic frame* can be used in the following way.

Organization is theater: Various actors play out the drama inside the organization, while outside audiences form impressions based on what they see occurring onstage. Problems arise when actors play their parts badly, when symbols lose their meaning, when ceremonies and rituals lose their potency. Improvements in rebuilding the expressive or spiritual side of organizations come through the use of symbol, myth, or magic.

This case study on reforming the prison system provides an opportunity to view a public agency through the symbolic frame and to develop an appropriate course of action.

THE CASE

In our state, the prison system has been the target of fierce public commentary. The courts continue to incarcerate criminals, stuffing more into an already overcrowded system, while demanding reform and attention to prisoner rights. The legislature, faced with shrinking revenues, has reduced the overall budget, vetoing funds for a new facility. Additionally, many legislators are feeling pressure from their constituents' calls for prison and criminal justice reform; consequently, legislative panels are reviewing all prison and justice system procedures. The media has "villainized" the prison system through several news reports following crimes committed by former inmates. The system has been challenged for violating prisoner rights by the American Civil Liberties Union (ACLU), accusing the system of doubling prison population without increasing prison capacity. The warden of the largest facility recently made a public address in which he criticized the state prison system for waste and abuse of funds, personnel cutbacks, and inadequate training for prison guards and employees. Guards and employees have unionized and threaten to strike if their demands for shorter hours, higher wages, increased prison security, and other reforms are not met. Inmate unrest portends violence, and their leaders are demanding more "ethnic" guards, better (adequate) health care, isolation from HIV-positive inmates, and additional visitation rights for family members.

Several issues this past year have further fueled the debate for change. First, several inmates and their family members have charged that parole board members accept bribes for arranging early release.

Second, the federal prison system has sent a number of foreign nationals convicted of immigration fraud and other crimes to state prisons. Third, a prisoner released through an administrative error committed a series of rapes, and then raped and killed a nine-year-old girl. One television station investigation discovered 35 such errors in a 12-month period, and half of the inmates released had already committed crimes again. Fourth, several inmate epidemics verified the substandard quality of health care in the system.

∽∾o∾∾

INSTRUCTIONS AND QUESTIONS

You have lived in this state for five years and have recently retired as city manager in the capital city. You are asked to take a temporary assignment of two to three years as Director of Prisons to initiate prison reforms. You are well known in the state as a tough but fair administrator with a strong code of professional ethics. You have good political connections. You will be given the support necessary to make changes. After a meeting with the governor, you agree to accept the assignment.

The Governor's mandate to you is to restore confidence in the system as quickly as possible. To tackle this assignment, you will need to act in all four frames; however, the Governor asks for you to develop a written plan for using the symbolic frame. She identifies the major constituencies as the media (television, radio, print media); the legislature; two liberal statewide public advocacy groups; a conservative prison reform group; the prison guard's union; taxpayers in general; a statewide victims' rights group; and the prison board.

Develop a plan of action using the symbolic frame that addresses all of these constituencies. This task must be completed within your first 30 days on the job.

25

Environmental Quality

The Western State Office of Environmental Quality (OEQ) has been in existence for some 15 years. Its primary functions have revolved around three principal duties: (1) ensuring that Western State's air and water quality meet federally mandated guidelines; (2) developing ongoing state plans to improve water quality, especially near the rivers and streams frequented by tourists but utilized as well by the state's three biggest employers—the coal companies that move their residue and waste through those waters; and (3) being responsive to citizen needs and desires on environmental quality.

For most of the department's 15-year history, the agency was known for its skill at balancing the first two elements of its mission; but the Western State Legislature has been putting increasing pressure on the third leg of the agency's mission. Specifically, the agency is criticized for its "narrow definition" of its role and of its seeming unwillingness to move beyond "traditional" clients, that is, environmental, producer, and federal government.

∽○∾

INSTRUCTIONS AND QUESTIONS

The new Director wants to work on expanding the agency's goals and mission but does not want to disturb the high level of effectiveness and efficiency with which the department operates.

Explain in detail how the Western State OEQ can meet the requirements of "excellence" while expanding its basic mission and focus.

26

Mixed Effects of a Demonstration Project

The following case describes the evaluation of a multiyear, multimillion-dollar government experiment. The demonstration project was implemented in order to test the effectiveness of potential modifications of an existing human resource system.

THE DEMONSTRATION PROJECT

Recent reports have suggested that the personnel recruitment and selection procedures employed by the federal government hinder the public sector's ability to recruit and select high-quality individuals. In many cases, qualified job candidates forgo promising job opportunities simply to avoid the complexity and slow pace associated with the federal hiring process. Similarly, hiring officials within the government feel the process is overly complex and time-consuming. They believe it constrains their ability to make decisions and initiate innovative approaches to local situations.

The Former System

The standard recruitment and selection process distances the hiring official from the applicant pool—in part, to protect merit system principles. These principles require that positions be filled through fair and open competition without regard to political affiliation or other nonmerit factors. When a position opens at a particular site, a notice of the opening and a list of the job qualifications are submitted to the central office by the official. The applicants on a central register of names are rated and ranked for the position on the basis of standardized test scores and job-related criteria. A certificate list is then returned to the hiring official, who may select any of the top three available individuals. The "cert list" generally contains the names of more than three individuals to ensure that the number of available candidates is adequate for the manager to make a choice. If the hiring official wishes to select a candidate who is not among the top three candidates, then he or she must show that one of the top three is ineligible.

While hiring officials make the final selection, they have little control over who appears on the cert list. The ratings and ranks are completed by clerks in the central office who may understand little or nothing about the position in question. This is particularly true when the position is in a highly specialized or scientific field. Further, the applicants on the cert list may not be interested in the position. While each has applied for federal employment, they may not want to work in a particular unit, or be interested in relocating to a given geographic region. Finally, some or all of the applicants on the cert list may no longer be available. Because applicants' names may remain on a register for a year or more, many of them may have accepted other positions long before the list is even assembled. Thus, while the standard recruitment and selection procedures protect merit principles through centralized responsibility for identifying pools of qualified candidates, they limit the hiring official's influence over the composition of the applicant pool, the criteria by which applicants are evaluated, and the ordering of candidates.

One method of resolving these issues was a less centralized method of recruitment and selection. However, before this system was permanently installed it was initially implemented as a short-term demonstration project.

Demonstration Project Goals and Initiatives

The purpose of the demonstration project was to develop a recruitment and selection program for new hires that is flexible and responsive to local recruitment needs and which will facilitate the attainment of a quality workforce reflective of society. In addition, it was intended to enhance the federal government's ability to compete with the private sector for qualified individuals. The demonstration project consists of four discrete components or initiatives: (a) an alternative candidate assessment method using categorical grouping rather than the traditional rating and ranking; (b) delegated authority to determine a shortage category, for which direct hiring authority is approved; (c) the option to award monetary recruitment incentives; and (d) the option to reimburse relocation travel and transportation expenses.

In sum, the demonstration initiatives afford the local hiring official much greater control over the recruitment and selection processes. Rather than depending upon a centralized authority, agency officials can customize the recruitment process to fit the nature and requirements of the position. Hiring officials at the local level are authorized to use all available recruitment sources to develop a pool of applicants and may determine which of these sources is most suitable for the particular position to be filled. For example, officials may decide to capitalize on the local labor pool by advertising in local papers for an administrative assistant position. Alternatively, they may wish to embark on a national search for a highly specialized position by announcing the opening in a targeted set of journals and periodicals. The hiring official might also choose to utilize professional networks or to contact respected graduate programs in order to identify highly qualified candidates.

Once a group of applicants has been recruited, individuals are categorized into quality and eligible groups. Applicants are assigned to the quality group on the basis of above-average educational achievement, job-related quality experience, and/or high ability. The hiring official may also specify selective placement factors that ensure applicants in the quality group have the training and experience necessary to successfully perform the job. Any candidate assigned to the quality group might be selected. Thus, the quality grouping process does not include the traditional "rule of three." Candidates who do not fall into the quality group but who pass minimum qualifications standards are assigned to the "eligible group." If the quality group is not sufficiently large, the eligible group also may be referred to the manager.

The recruitment incentives and the relocation expense components of the demonstration project were intended to enhance the ability of the agency to compete with other employers for individuals with desired skills. These incentives are drawn from the local unit's operating budget and can be used at local discretion. In some cases, the awards allow the hiring official to compensate for the disparity between public and private sector salaries in tight labor markets. In other cases, they might be used to "lure" highly qualified individuals away from positions with private employers.

The demonstration project operated under the constraint that it not adversely affect the fair representation of protected groups in the workforce. Indeed, the project's initiatives may provide a powerful tool for increasing social representation. The ability to conduct targeted recruitment efforts and to use recruitment incentives, together with the greater availability of candidates under the categorical grouping procedure, might improve the ability of hiring officials to attract highly qualified women, minorities, and individuals with disabilities into the workforce.

Site History

The Ecology Research Service (ERS) was one of the agencies chosen to participate in the demonstration project. It is a relatively large agency with approximately 30,000 permanent employees, an annual budget in excess of one billion dollars, and approximately 150 sites spread across the country. The agency manages and protects a vast array of natural resources and maintains applied research programs in a number of laboratories and research centers. In many respects the ERS has a quasi-military character and has traditionally demonstrated a tendency to promote from within. That is, hiring officials have long shown a preference of hiring individuals "who have come up through the ranks." In recent years, this has lead to concern over the homogeneity of the agency's workforce. The basic experimental design of the demonstration project involved the random assignment of sites, with size and location constraints, to experimental (DEMO) and comparison conditions. The demonstration initiatives were implemented in approximately 70 experimental sites, while the remaining sites were required to continue using the standard recruitment and selection processes.

The Blackwater Site

The Blackwater site was selected as one DEMO site. It is located in a rural region of the Southeast, about two and a half hours outside of the nearest urban area. The site encompasses both the Blackwater Reservoir Recreational Park and the Blackwater Biological Laboratory. The park covers a large geographic area and is the largest employer in the local labor market. Although the Blackwater Biological Laboratory is located within the park, it is an administratively distinct unit within the agency. The laboratory was established in 1965, has maintained a strong research program in applied ecology, and is staffed by more than 30 employees.

Blackwater's research personnel had for years been very interested in the prospect of having more influence in the site's selection process owing to a cynicism about the home office's ability to effectively select personnel for their site. Blackwater officials felt that only they really knew their needs, their community, and their work environment. How could someone or something hundreds of miles away select people for them?

Administrative Officer

Dr. Jordan Smith had been the hiring officer at Blackwater for about 10 years and had often felt his efforts to recruit top scientists to his office were frustrated by the mandates of the home office. His cynicism was often conveyed to his co-workers at the site during lunches and informal monthly meetings. Jordan and the research scientists at the site frequently identified potential co-workers when attending conferences. However, other private organizations were usually able to steal these prospects. Jordan saw the DEMO hiring initiatives as providing his site greater leverage in the recruitment process. Finally, he believed he would be able to steal someone else's hires.

Jordan attended the training session on the demonstration project that was held prior to its implementation. He actively participated in sessions and maintained close contact with fellow hiring officers at other DEMO sites. He was excited about his site's new ability both to recruit and hire locally, and to offer recruitment incentives like relocation expenses and cash bonuses. He was concerned, however, about initiatives to diversify the agency. Jordan wasn't sure how personnel at his site would react, but he didn't worry about it. He didn't know of any minorities interested in his field. After all, he generally searched for scientists. Very few women were interested in this type of work, Jordan believed; and he doubted there were any minority applicants.

Research Scientists

Jordan was responsible for hiring personnel and managing the Blackwater site. Basically, he managed the work of his administrative assistant and three research scientists. Each of the research scientists was responsible for a staff comprised of research assistants. Jordan has had a long and comfortable relationship with each of the scientists mostly because they have so much in common.

Dr. Jack Thomas had spent all of his career with the agency, 12 of those years at Blackwater. He enjoyed his work and the relationships that he had established with his co-workers. He looked forward to the recognition Blackwater would receive as a demonstration site. He knew that once the word was out about Blackwater's ability to function as a smooth-running machine, he would be the envy of his colleagues at other sites in the agency.

Dr. Joshua Toombs worked in the private sector before moving to Blackwater. His career change was prompted by his need to work in an environment that he viewed as "less political" and "more scientific." His three years in the private sector had made him suspicious of personnel interventions like the demonstration project. He was happy with the rule of three and felt that choosing personnel based upon their performance on a standardized test ensured a fair and bias-free process.

Dr. Jill Pettaway was the only female professional at the site. She began her tenure at the site fresh out of graduate school. Her father had been a research scientist at another site in their region, and she grew up expecting to have the same experiences that he had told her about. However, her experiences in graduate school and at Blackwater had been dramatically different. It was almost a year before Jack and Joshua would recognize her as a colleague. Rather than receive mentoring or advice from senior colleagues as her male classmates had received at other sites, Jill was forced to go it alone. She knew from Jack and Joshua's patronizing behavior that they felt she was less qualified than they. However, she had passed the same test that they had in order to be hired. She chose to work harder and longer than they did in order to prove her worth. Also, along the way she learned to "fit in." Eventually, the three scientists learned to coexist.

YEARLY FOCUS GROUP DATA

Every year of the demonstration project, evaluation teams (usually two evaluators) visited a small sample of the DEMO and control sites. Blackwater was chosen to be one of those demonstration sites that would receive a yearly visit by the evaluation team. These visits were designed to monitor local events that may influence the effectiveness of the demonstration project. Sites varied in their receptiveness to these yearly visits.

Year One

The first year, the visit to Blackwater took place only one month after the demonstration project was implemented. Jordan had recently returned from training and had just briefed his personnel on the demonstration project the week before the evaluation team arrived.

Interview with Senior Personnel Officer

The interview with Jordan was pleasant but short. He seemed to believe that the evaluation team was there to test his knowledge of the demonstration authority. Every time the evaluation team inquired about his site and the reactions of his personnel to the initiatives he was determined to give a factual response directed at the intricacies of the project.

Focus Group with Site Personnel

Personnel were excited about the implementation of DEMO at their site. They asked the interviewers several questions about how other sites were coping with this new opportunity. They were confident that their site would prove to be the "best" demonstration site of all 25. Although the interviewers explained that this was not a competition, the incumbents still maintained a "we're the best" attitude. Both Jack and Joshua had already alerted their former graduate school advisors and classmates of the new hiring initiative with the hopes of getting some more "quality people like us" on board at Blackwater. No mention was ever made of the monetary incentives or diversity initiatives. Jill had very little to say. When she did speak, she often just repeated what Jack or Joshua had mentioned previously.

Year Two

During year two the evaluation team visited Blackwater. The hiring official, Jordan, had used DEMO to hire Francine. She joined carryovers Jack and Joshua.

Interview with Senior Personnel Officer

Jordan was anxious to meet with the evaluation team. In fact, he had so much to report that their meeting with him delayed the team's scheduled meeting with the pre-DEMO scientists. Jordan reported that Jill unexpectedly left Blackwater, citing a "poor work climate." Jordan didn't seem to understand what that meant and was sad to see Jill leave because she was their only female scientist. However, he had been excited to finally get an opportunity to use the demonstration project authority.

He felt the DEMO authority worked well and that he was able to attract two exceptional candidates; one was even a minority woman,

Francine. He knew that attracting minorities was one of the goals of DEMO and that it would be quite a feather in his cap if Francine came aboard. It took a great deal of negotiating with Francine, but he was finally able to "snag her." It seemed as though Francine had several good offers from both the public and private sectors, and Jordan felt that DEMO, especially in providing authority for a cash bonus as well as relocation expenses, really helped him recruit a minority female.

Focus group with Pre-DEMO Personnel

The evaluation team met with Jack and Joshua immediately after their meeting with Jordan. The evaluators were intrigued by the differences in tone between the two meetings. Whereas Jordan's meeting was upbeat and celebratory, the meeting with Joshua and Jack seemed tense and angry.

Both Joshua and Jack seemed unhappy with the demonstration project. They had both gone through a lot to notify good candidates about the vacancy, and were shocked that Jordan didn't choose to hire "their guys." Like Francine, both of their candidates had made it into the quality group. The carryover scientists both believed that if the ranking system had been in place, Francine would have been at the bottom of the quality group. However, DEMO permitted hiring officers the ability to use their discretion and hire any of the "quality" candidates. Joshua and Jack were both angered that Francine was hired. They suspected that Jordan hired her for political reasons and to boost his image in the agency. Joshua was especially upset that "affirmative action was going to ruin what we've had at this site." When asked to explain, he indicated that he felt the site's reputation and productivity would eventually be tarnished. Jack also seemed angered that Francine was rumored to have received a $10,000 signing bonus as well as relocation expenses. He reported that no one had offered these things to him, and said "obviously I am better than her."

Interview with the Sole DEMO Hire

The interview with Francine was difficult. She seemed disinterested and unattached to the site. When asked how it felt to be the first DEMO hire at Blackwater, she responded that it was difficult but that it was nothing she hadn't faced before or wouldn't have to deal with in the future.

Blackwater was more of the same; Francine explained that regardless of her education or credentials, none of her previous employers, co-workers, or classmates ever assumed that she was really qualified.

The first time this had happened to her was when she went to college. At the time, she was angry and depressed at the other students' assumptions concerning how she was admitted and about her competence. She explained that rather than focusing on her schoolwork, she spent her time in and out of class trying to prove her worth—at the expense of her grades and well-being. Francine said she benefited from that experience and that she learned to be less concerned with what others thought of her and to focus more on what she was attempting to achieve.

Later, in graduate school as well as on summer jobs and internships, Francine was confronted with similar issues but didn't allow them to bother her. She knew that this strategy often resulted in her being labeled "aloof and difficult," but she saw that strategy as necessary to accomplishing her goals. Isolation was a small price to pay for her to perform up to her potential. She wondered why no one ever questioned the selection or competence of her classmates or colleagues.

Year Three

Year three was the last year of evaluation site visits.

Interview with the Senior Personnel Officer

Jordan clearly seemed happy that the demonstration period was coming to an end. Although DEMO made his job more important and visible to the agency, it also caused interpersonal problems at work. He realized that when Jill cited "climate" problems as her reason for leaving, she was probably right. Joshua and Jack constantly complained about Francine—not really her work, but her "attitude." It had finally reached the point where Joshua and Jack worked together, and Francine worked on her own projects. Jordan knew that Joshua and Jack really wanted him fired for hiring Francine, but, because of his tenure with the agency, that it was unlikely.

When the agency gave Jordan the opportunity to expand his site, he decided that he would do things right this time. Jordan said, "The quality group was comprised of a woman, a man, and a minority woman, all very similarly qualified; I wasn't going to make the same mistake again." Jordan hired the male candidate—Jake.

Focus Group with Pre-DEMO Personnel

Joshua and Jack seemed less confrontational than at the second-year meeting. They still seemed to mourn the opportunity that Francine blocked, but they were happy to get someone "normal like Jake." Both went on and on about how Jake was a regular kind of guy you could work with, go fishing with, and have a beer with. Both brought Jake onto their projects and introduced him to colleagues at conferences and scientific meetings. They felt Jake would be with the agency for years to come.

Focus Group with DEMO Hires

Jake and Francine met with the evaluation team together. The team was surprised by how little Jake and Francine knew of each other. They had never seemed to discuss their research or education, although they seemed to share many of the same interests and contacts. Francine seemed to be off doing her own thing, while Jake's time was spent with either Joshua or Jack. Both seemed pleased with the manner in which they were recruited as well as with the packages they were offered. When asked about how they felt the demonstration project influenced their work environment, Francine did not respond. Jake indicated that he felt that the research team was a warm, supportive group and was highly collaborative. He didn't know if that was due to DEMO or not.

∽o∾

INSTRUCTIONS AND QUESTIONS

1. Given the information provided, identify the major barriers to the effective implementation of DEMO at this site.
2. In what ways could the demonstration project be modified so that it could retain its initial goals yet reduce the occurrence of interpersonal problems such as those that took place at the Blackwater site?

PART FIVE

Personnel and Human Resource Issues

		Page
27.	A Supervisor for Unit II	141
28.	Affirmative Action in Hamilton County	144
29.	HIV and Employee Rights	150
30.	Performance Evaluation and Organizational Rigidity	153
31.	The Police Captain Dilemma	158
32.	Reasonable Accommodation	160
33.	A Subordinate's Homophobia	163

27

A Supervisor for Unit II

There is a substantial increase in the volume of work in the division you head, Administrative/Technical. This work increase results in a management survey designed to provide better utilization of personnel. One recommendation calls for the creation of two new units, to be made up of personnel specialized in the handling of certain kinds of cases.

This recommendation is approved by your bosses, and you, as chief of the division, are told to go ahead and fill the two positions. The two units are to be made up of GS-13s and GS-14s, with a GS-15 in charge. One unit poses no problems: The person selected is clearly well qualified for the job and is one of the most experienced people in the organization. He is well thought of by both supervisors and subordinates.

In Unit II, however, the case is not as clear-cut. Following are the leading candidates:

- *George Wilson* has been with Administrative/Technical for 16 years, has both a legal and accounting background, and is the most senior person available. He is regarded as a good technical man for detail. It pains Wilson to let a case leave him unless it reflects the best possible thinking he can give it. This means, of course, that he is limited in the number of cases he can handle, although he puts in a fair amount of overtime.

  His superiors know that when they get a recommendation from Wilson they can depend on it.

  WIlson also has the respect of his associates, but they do not find it easy to work with him. When they have been members of task forces of which he has been in charge, they have felt that he required too much of them, took too great an interest in the details of the job, and was likely to tell them precisely how to go about it.

- *Wendell Rogers* is 10 years younger than Wilson and has had his GS-14 rating only six months. He is a goal setter who believes in getting the job done. Twice in the past two years, however, he has pushed ahead faster than the information he had would warrant. Consequently, major errors were made. One of these errors was caught before it left Administrative/Technical, so no harm was done. But the other error resulted in considerable controversy—in which the agency's chief executive himself became involved. In fairness to Rogers, it should be noted that both these errors were made in work done by subordinates that he had not examined carefully. Rogers is well liked by his associates and would be a popular choice for unit head.

- *Marbury Madison* had been in Administrative/Technical earlier in his career, but he is now in the San Francisco region where he has been on special assignment for the past two years, working on a team installing a computer system. He has had a GS-14 rating for three years and is regarded by those at agency headquarters as well qualified for the position. Madison also has the respect of those who have worked with him, although he is not regarded as GS-16 talent. Madison and his wife both like living in San Francisco, where they recently bought a house. They do not really want to return to Washington, but they might be persuaded to do so if they felt they were badly needed.

- *Hannah Hyde*, the fourth possibility for the position, has spent most of her career in another area of Administrative/Technical, but she has handled some of the same kinds of cases that would be given to the new unit she might head. However, the general feeling is that it would take her at least six months to get on top of the job. There is some reason to believe that her promotion would cause resentment by division members because an "outsider" was brought in. Hyde also believes that she has a good chance for promotion within a few months where she is now.

Several added factors that may influence the selection should be noted. Although the Deputy Administrator of your agency is aware that Wilson is likely to be tough on his subordinates, he has high respect for Wilson's ability on technical matters. As for Rogers, there is some fear in the front office that he may not be careful enough with detail, although they admit that this opinion is based on only the two cases in which errors were made.

The Personnel Office, on the other hand, prefers a good supervisor who can bring his subordinates along; they are inclined toward Rogers.

Whatever is done, Personnel urges that no appointment be made on an "acting" basis.

The Training Division points out that Madison has not been through its management training programs. Training does not want to see anyone given a job of this nature who has not participated in its programs, although Training does not denigrate Madison's abilities. All other possible promotees have been through these programs.

∽◦∾

INSTRUCTIONS AND QUESTIONS

As chief of the division you are expected to make a choice. You know that your decision is being watched with a great deal of interest by all concerned.

1. How do you decide?
2. Why?

28

Affirmative Action in Hamilton County

Luther Gritsch recently moves from Personnel to the Human Rights Division (HRD) of his federal agency, with enthusiasm. He accepts the change in location that is offered to him to become a regional HRD representative. Though gaining nothing in salary, losing a little in terms of office comforts, and breaking about even on an exchange of residences, Luther and his wife, Maureen, are excited about the new position with HRD. There is real substance to Luther's enthusiasm. Luther enjoys working with people younger than himself, both because they respond to his energy and because they are more likely than Luther's peers or superiors to share his political and social views. He looks forward to traveling around the new region and to taking Maureen along—at least until she is ready to resume her career when they are well settled in. And, Luther hopes that HRD can provide an example in this region of what can be throughout the agency. He has programmatic aspirations, not just case-processing ones.

Basically, Luther likes HRD's mission. HRD is in charge of affirmative action plans. The agency requires that grant recipients certify that they are in compliance with antidiscrimination statutes and regulations, and that they submit an acceptable affirmative action plan regarding hiring and promotion. HRD also handles complaints from the department's grantees as well as from individuals within the department.

Moreover, the HRD job will increase his contact with young people, who, in Luther's department, are the most turned on by "human rights."

In getting oriented to the new job and new region, Luther visits a number of cities and counties that have submitted applications for funds. Luther accompanies Martin Donnelly, from one of the program offices, on such a visit to Hamilton County. As they pass from office to office in the county courthouse and office building, Luther is able to observe day-to-day county activities and personnel practices.

Later, he and Martin lunch with a group of employees in the cafeteria. As they talk, they are joined by Della Lenhardt, who is attracted by their animated discussion of women's rights. When she learns that Luther is from the HRD of a federal department, she decides to move the discussion from generalities to specifics.

"Let me tell you about how women are treated here," she says. "I'm a Grade 6 secretary, and I've worked for Mal Porterfield for seven years, since I graduated from Hamilton State. Every time I try to get a promotion, I get some damn fool excuse. Just a few months ago, when the Manpower grant came through, I asked Porterfield if I could be considered for one of the field representative jobs. That's a Grade 9 job, and I had the degree in the right field, because the specs said someone with a social science or labor relations degree, and I took my degree in sociology.

"Porterfield told me that they could not consider me for the job because it involved travel," Della concludes.

"Because the job requires travel?" Luther asks.

"Yes," Della Lenhardt replies. "I asked him to let me make an application, but he said it just made no sense. He couldn't consider any woman for the job because of the travel, and he didn't want to have to process the papers for me since he couldn't hire me, even if he wanted to. He told me that the department appreciated my dedication and efficiency and would seek to find a proper way to reward my work."

Luther is intrigued. "What did you do then?"

"What *could* I do? The last female who challenged Porterfield had her job abolished and was offered nothing better than a clerical job in Rydersville."

"What's Rydersville?" Luther asks.

"That's the county jail farm, about 40 miles south of here on Old State Route 107," someone offers.

"Yeah, it's about a 60-minute drive on a good day, and you should see the place. It may be pretty at that end of the country, but what a dump to work in!" someone else says.

The employees begin breaking up to go back to work. Luther is disturbed by what he hears at lunch and wants to know more. He asks Donnelly if they can stop by the Personnel Office after their first afternoon meeting. Donnelly arranges a visit with Paul Joyner, the Deputy Personnel Director, at 2:15. When they get to Joyner's office, he is not there. After a 20-minute wait, Joyner flashes in, breathless, and apologizes for keeping them waiting. "But I can't stay very long. I have to make a presentation to the County Board at 2:40 and can't hold them up. What is it you wanted to know?"

Surprised by this brusque treatment, Luther blurts out, "Do you have an affirmative action plan in this county?" He had planned to be more subtle, but that is the way it came out.

Joyner seems almost offended. "Of course we do. We drafted one up last year when a group of women got together and complained about hiring practices or some such thing. Ask my girl for a copy on your way out," Joyner concludes. "She'll have one somewhere. Sorry to be so abrupt, but I really must run over to the courthouse. If there's anything else I can do, just give me a call. Mrs. Aldrich will help you find your way out. Really sorry for the rush."

And Joyner is gone as swiftly as he came.

Luther and Martin Donnelly sit and stare at Joyner's empty chair. Donnelly just shakes his head and exhales a long "Wow!"

Luther looks at Donnelly and says: "Is that the way the department gets treated in this region? This place needs some changes. Let's get a copy of that plan. I'd love to see it. I guess Mrs. Aldrich is his 'girl' in the outer office."

"Don't get so excited. This place isn't so bad," Donnelly says.

"We'll see about that," Luther replies.

Mrs. Aldrich asks Luther and Donnelly to have a seat while she searches for a copy of the affirmative action plan. She is gone for 10 or 15 minutes before returning with a slightly worn copy. "I'm sorry it took so long," she apologizes. "I finally borrowed a copy from Mrs. Kingston in the Assessor's Office. Being one of our new black employees, she's really interested in these matters. Of course we have lots of them in the Highway Department, but not here in the county offices. We don't have many in this county anyway, but we try to be fair. Some of them aren't really qualified, but we all try to do our little part to help out."

"How long have you worked for the county, Mrs. Aldrich?" Luther asks.

"Almost 20 years, ever since my children grew up," Mrs. Aldrich replies. "I worked for Mr. Porterfield, before he became Human Services Director, and before that for 10 years in Purchasing. Mr. Joyner, he seems awfully stern sometimes, but he's really nice when you get to know him."

"Have you ever thought of doing something more than secretarial work, Mrs. Aldrich?" Luther asks.

"Hey Luther, we really ought to get going if we're going to make the four o'clock flight," Donnelly interjects as he picks up Luther's briefcase and opens the office door. "If we miss that one we'll be here overnight."

"I guess I'll have to be going; can I return the affirmative action plan back by mail?" Luther asks of Mrs. Aldrich.

"Perhaps it would be better if I had Mr. Joyner send you a clean copy. This is Mrs. Kingston's, you know, and I promised to bring it back."

"Well, thank you for your time, Mrs. Aldrich. I'm sure I'll see you on my next visit. Thank you very much."

Upon returning from Hamilton County, Luther spends two days working on a trip report. In it, he gives a detailed account of what he observed in Hamilton County, emphasizing those weaknesses in the county's affirmative action "plan" that had been evident even in a once-over. He recommends that the Hamilton County grant application be held up pending a thorough review of the county's personnel practices and the submission by the county personnel office of an affirmative action plan "with teeth in it." He sends his report to the HRD office in Washington, with copies going to the regional director, his own supervisor, and the assistant regional director for administration.

Luther's supervisor, Jesse Weldon, praises the report but criticizes Luther for sending it "upstairs" without approval. He tells Luther that HRD is new—both as a unit and as a concept—and that it has to be very careful.

Weldon suggests that Luther write to Della Lenhardt—or better still, call her—and explain the options provided in the law enabling her to make a complaint at the state level or with the federal Equal Employment Opportunity Commission (EEOC). But, Weldon concludes, "though I wish you had come to me before raising the issue higher, we'll try and see if we can't do something about Hamilton County. Maybe we can at least slow them down and make them think."

Weldon sets up a meeting with the assistant regional director for administration. He also calls Martin Donnelly's boss and talks him into sending a brief, innocuous letter informing Mal Porterfield that the regional office wishes to examine their affirmative action proposal more carefully, now that additional information has been gained from the site visit.

It is two weeks before Weldon and Luther get to see the assistant regional director. After an exchange of pleasantries and a conversation about business in general, the assistant regional director takes both

Luther's report and a larger document from a locked desk drawer. "This is about Hamilton County and Mal Porterfield, right? Good man, Mal. Known him for a long time. He has never misspent a penny of federal money, not a penny."

"I'm sure he is a good man, sir," Luther replies. "But we are here because of his personnel policies, rather than his financial policies. I feel that his department, and possibly the entire county government, is in gross and wholesale violation of the law regarding minority and women's employment."

"Hamilton County? What's their percentage minority anyway, Jess?" the assistant regional director asks.

"Four percent in the county, but closer to 20 percent in the county seat," is the reply.

"There's not a lot you can do about that, is there?" he asks. "We have counties that are 20 and 30 percent minority in this region. As for the women's thing, there's been a lot of unemployment down there. I don't want to hold up a proposal like this for that," the assistant director explains as he flashes the other, larger document he had removed from his desk. "This kind of thing can create jobs. There's no point in making jobs into musical chairs."

Luther agrees. "I understand that, sir, but we do have laws to enforce."

"And we have money to move out and people who really want to see us move it," the assistant regional director responds. "You fellows are doing important work, don't get me wrong. But, there are other objectives for this department as well. This grant proposal is going to be approved, but I want you to keep an eye on Hamilton County and let me know if you have any more trouble with them."

"Is there any chance it could be held up for a few more weeks, just to make them think a little?" Weldon asks.

"Be reasonable, Jess," the assistant director counsels. "You know they have an approved affirmative action plan. They had it approved in Washington over a year ago. I wouldn't hold up anything this important just on the basis of a site visit and one report. If that's your game, you're going to have to be a lot more convincing than this."

"But sir," Luther says excitedly, "just look at the examples in my report. If I could find so much in just a brief visit, imagine what must be going on there!"

∽o∾
INSTRUCTIONS AND QUESTIONS

1. What is your assessment about what's really going on in Hamilton County?
2. Did Luther "overreact?" How else could he have proceeded?
3. If you were Luther, what would you do next?

29

HIV and Employee Rights

Paul Johnson is the city manager of Rockland, a growing community of 18,000 located 14 miles from the state's largest metropolitan area. Johnson, 36, has been working in city government for 11 years, and is a graduate of the state's only accredited public administration program. He considers himself a good leader who is especially adept at resolving conflicts.

Recently, David Spencer, head of the parks and recreation department, informed Johnson that one of the department's employees, Jesse Neighbors, has been complaining of fatigue and loss of weight and has not reported for work the past week.

Neighbors, 38, is openly homosexual, and speculation within the department, according to Spencer, is that Neighbors has AIDS. "After all," he told Johnson, "everybody knew that the guy was gay when he hired on. When he comes down sick, it's only logical that the guys assume he has AIDS. Some of them probably won't be too thrilled about working with him when he comes back."

Johnson acknowledged that Neighbors could have contracted HIV, but suggested other possibilities. "Hell, David, the guy could have heart disease or emphysema," Johnson said. "He smokes two packs a day. There's no need to fear the worst. We'll deal with the situation when Jesse comes back to work."

Four days later, Neighbors called Johnson to tell him that he, Neighbors, had received doctor's clearance to return to work. During the course of the conversation, Neighbors said that he had tested positive for HIV, and he speculated on how that would affect his ability to work with the other employees in parks and recreation. Johnson said that he was more concerned about Neighbors' ability to function effectively on the job. Neighbors assured Johnson that he was physically able to perform his work, but he said he might occasionally need some personal time for a doctor's appointment.

After talking to Neighbors, Johnson called the city attorney, David Barnes, and told him about the situation, without mentioning Neighbors's name. Johnson was specifically interested in how to deal with the possibility that some employees would be reluctant to work with a person they suspected of having AIDS, but he also speculated about what obligations the city may have to its employees concerning HIV-positive workers. He specifically asked whether the city would be liable if a city employee contracted the virus while working with an HIV-positive city employee.

Barnes told Johnson that he would have to do some research to determine how the courts have ruled in similar cases. Meanwhile, he advised the city manager to keep the knowledge of Neighbors's condition confidential, and to meet with the employee's supervisor before the employee's return in an effort to head off speculation.

Johnson called Spencer and asked him to meet with him at three o'clock that afternoon. When the meeting began, Johnson told Spencer that Neighbors would be coming back to work the following day. "His doctor cleared him for work, and Jesse says he's okay. That's really all I can tell you. I expect your employees to treat Jesse the same as they do anybody who's returning to work after an illness. If there's any talk about refusing to work with him because they suspect he has AIDS, I want you to call me." Spencer said he'd keep Johnson apprised of the situation.

Neighbors's first day back was uneventful, but, on the morning of the second day, a small group of workers from the department, led by Charley Wetherby, came to Spencer to say that they suspected that Neighbors had AIDS; they asked for assurance that they wouldn't be assigned to his detail. Wetherby also told Spencer that he thought the employees in the department deserved to know if Neighbors had contracted AIDS.

Spencer told Wetherby that Neighbors's medical condition was confidential and refused to guarantee that the men wouldn't have to work with Neighbors. The controversy remained unresolved when the meeting ended. Spencer then called Johnson to tell him of the potential crisis. Johnson told Spencer to schedule a meeting with Wetherby and his group that afternoon at 4:30 P.M. in Spencer's office.

∽o∾

INSTRUCTIONS AND QUESTIONS

1. What are Johnson's options in dealing with the possibility that Wetherby and his men will refuse to work with Neighbors?
2. Could this situation have been avoided if the city had instituted an AIDS policy and an AIDS education program for its employees?
3. Do Neighbors's co-workers have a right to know whether he is infected with HIV? Should Neighbors tell them?
4. Is Johnson under any obligation to accommodate Neighbors's condition or even retain him as an employee in light of his condition?

30

Performance Evaluation and Organizational Rigidity

It is only 10:00 A.M., and Jim Daniels has already had four cups of coffee and attended three meetings. His desk is still piled high with paper-work, and tomorrow will be Friday, his last workday before the start of two weeks of long-awaited vacation. He puts aside the report he is read-ing and reflects upon some of the problems in his organization that have arisen or intensified during the past month. He thinks for a few minutes and then says to himself: "How can I afford to go away at such a critical time?"

Most people would agree that Jim Daniels had started a brilliant mil-itary career. He had performed well in every assignment given to him from the very beginning and had been awarded outstanding ratings on all past performance evaluations. Twice he had been promoted ahead of his contemporaries, and he now holds the rank of lieutenant colonel.

In his present assignment, Jim is commander of a selectively staffed Air Force squadron that flies aircraft with a unique mission. When Jim was a captain six years ago, he had applied and competed for an as-signment in this prestigious unit; like many other members of the squadron, he was promoted early and sent to a military school for promising command and staff officers. Following one year of school, he spent two years on the headquarters staff before assuming his present duties. Since he had previously served in this Air Force wing, Jim was already aware of most of his responsibilities when he arrived at the squadron. Equally important, he knew most of the people and tasks connected with the operation of his unit. All along, he had looked forward to this job and to working with high-caliber personnel. But a lot of things had changed since he had left for school, especially....

The phone rings. It is another young captain interested in applying for the unit's flying program. Jim only half-listens to this enthusiastic pilot tell about his background, but he does manage to give some answers to questions concerning the program scope and the duties and responsibilities that each new candidate will encounter. Jim's mind is still wandering back across the events of the morning when one last question from his caller brings him back to the phone conversation: "What sort of performance evaluation might I expect during my first year with your squadron?"

Performance evaluations! Performance evaluations! Everyone now seems concerned about performance evaluations. In fact, most of Jim's problems of the past week involved performance evaluations in some respect. Jim's first meeting of the day had been with the wing commander, the director of operations, and the director of training—a meeting dealing with past performance evaluations of new applicants for the unit flying program. The staff had prepared a personal folder for each candidate containing his personnel, flight, and physical records, letters of recommendation, and evaluation reports of the applicant's personal interviews with various members of the staff. The personnel records seem to have the most influence, since they contain personal data, previous duty assignments, and the individual's previous evaluations.

During the meeting with the wing commander, each participant studied each folder, asked questions of the staff, and completed a rank ordering of the most qualified candidates. Jim feels that the others gave too much weight to the performance evaluations and not enough attention to the other data available, especially the records of flight evaluations. The performance evaluations are too general for the purpose of evaluating flying accomplishments and skills, and are perhaps better suited to evaluating promotion and career potential. Jim wants to maintain the high personnel standards of his unit, but he needs more reassurance that those applicants with high performance evaluations are also highly skilled aviators. Moreover, he is concerned because he sees a trend developing—the number of highly qualified applicants has been decreasing over the past year since the Air Force instituted a new method of conducting performance evaluations for all officers. A few candidates chosen for the unit program had reconsidered accepting the assignment when they learned that, according to the new system, they would be competing against other members of the elite squadron for ratings, and it would not be possible for everyone to receive a top performance evaluation score.

In the second meeting, Jim got much data that reinforced his concern. He conferred with the unit personnel officer about finding replacements for the operations officer and the maintenance officer. These positions are about to become vacant due to personnel reassignments, and Jim was amazed to learn that nobody from the unit had volunteered for these two choice jobs. In his day, he would have jumped at the chance to gain additional experience in either of these two areas. Of course, it would have meant starting at the bottom again in a new organization, but the opportunity to learn new skills was tremendous. Jim was also surprised when the personnel officer told him that no one from his unit had made an application for a future assignment. During further discussion of the matter, Jim learned that better than half of his squadron had four or more years in their present assignment. Still more important, he learned that some people had turned down special assignments or schools. It looked as if some of the squadron members had staked organizational claims and were in the process of homesteading their assignments.

Jim's third meeting was with the wing administrative officer. The time was drawing near for completing performance evaluations for each of his squadron officers, and the administrative officer gave him a listing of pertinent data for each member to be evaluated plus a detailed briefing on the new evaluation procedures.

The wing administrative officer stressed one point about the performance evaluation procedures, a point that troubled Jim because he thought it would cause overcautious and shortsighted behavior among young officers: No more than 50 percent of the unit members would be able to receive the top two rating scores. The ratings assigned by the unit commander would be reviewed at two additional levels, and could be changed at either one or both levels. First, Jim would write the performance evaluation for each officer in his squadron and assign a rating. Second, the director of operations would review evaluations from his squadron, along with others from related units, and would assign a second rating, which could differ from the first. Finally, the wing commander would review and rate all the performance evaluations from all of the units. But the wing commander is still bound by the same quota constraints as are Jim and the director of operations: No more than 50 percent of those rated can receive the top two ratings, and no more than 20 percent of those can receive the top rating.

Jim picks up the report he was reading before the phone rang. He notes that better than 90 percent of the people who were eligible for promotion last cycle, and who received the top rating on their last performance evaluation, were in fact promoted. Additionally, almost 75 percent of those with the second-highest rating who were eligible for promotion were promoted. But less than 50 percent of those who received the third-highest rating were promoted; and less than 10 percent of the remaining eligible were promoted. There is little doubt that high performance evaluations are necessary for promotion, and the new system instituted throughout the Air Force makes virtual losers of 50 percent of the officers.

A knock on his door interrupts Jim's thought, and he answers cheerfully, "Come in." Captain John Douglas walks in and closes the door behind him. His face looks a bit strained, but his manner is calm and pleasant. Douglas is undoubtedly the best pilot in the organization, having been charged with instructing other pilots as well as training new members. He does his job extremely well and otherwise keeps to himself. Jim knows that this is no casual visit to shoot the breeze. After exchanging the pleasantries of the day, Douglas gets right to the point:

"Sir, we've got a big problem in our unit, and I don't know what to do about it. There used to be a great spirit of cooperation here; we would all help one another. Now people don't discuss much about their problems—I mean problems about how they fly or do their job. Maybe you've noticed the lack of exchange we've had lately at our crew meetings. It seems everyone is becoming secretive about recent experiences or about recent mistakes. They don't discuss much at all with the new trainees. They all seem to be running off doing their own little projects or blowing their own horn about their accomplishments. We just don't have the morale we used to have. I'm beginning to feel like a stranger in my own outfit."

Jim listens intently, for Douglas is usually in tune with what is going on in the unit. As the commander, Jim knows that declining morale is a recurring theme. Also, communications have occasionally been strained during the squadron meetings, and it is true that the unit sometimes acts as cliques or as individuals rather than as a team. For example, some tend to guard information that is valuable to others in the unit. On the surface, however, things seem to go well. For the most part, everyone is amiable. All the crew members did very well on their last flying evaluations, and the squadron received an outstanding rating on a no-notice inspection recently from headquarters. All the officers are professionals and perform their jobs in an exemplary fashion.

After Douglas leaves, Jim begins to think more about the upcoming performance evaluations of his unit, which will be due shortly after he returns from vacation. Somehow he will have to justify assigning less than a top rating to 80 percent of his officers—officers who had competed for this assignment and who were handpicked after careful consideration of their records. Jim begins to see the scope of the problem and once again thinks "How can I leave at a critical time like this?"

∽𝕠∾

INSTRUCTIONS AND QUESTIONS

You are Jim Daniels and are deeply concerned with the problems at hand. You are aware that the final selection of new personnel is now scheduled to be held while you are on vacation. You want to attend, but your wife is counting on the trip you have been planning.

You cannot afford to be without an operations officer and maintenance officer and would like to see experienced people from your unit take the jobs even though they might receive a lower performance evaluation in moving to an unfamiliar area. You believe it would not be in your unit's best interest for someone outside the organization to be assigned to the job.

There will be a squadron meeting the first day after you return from vacation.

1. What can you say or do to improve morale and communication?
2. Also, should you worry about completing the unit's performance evaluations?
3. How can you justify the ratings to your officers?
4. Prepare a memo to the wing commander outlining specific changes in the existing performance evaluation system that you recommend.

31

The Police Captain Dilemma

Karen Burchfield is the new city manager of Beacheaven. The City of Beacheaven has recently entered into a voluntary affirmative action plan aimed at increasing the representation of minorities and females at all workforce levels.

Beacheaven has had a checkered track record in hiring minorities and females. For example, the city's latest affirmative action report shows that African-American employees are concentrated among the lowest pay levels for all city employees. The police department has drawn particular attention. The Concerned Citizens Coalition (CCC) has recently publicized the fact that, while the percentage of African-American police officers is closely related to the percentage in the city (30 percent), there is a great gap in representation in the upper ranks of the department. The CCC has compiled the following data:

City of Beacheaven Current Police Department Staffing

Rank	African American	White	Total
Police Officer	98 (28%)	257 (72%)	355
Police Sergeant	12 (16%)	62 (84%)	74
Police Lieutenant	2 (11%)	16 (89%)	18
Police Captain	0 (0%)	4 (100%)	4
	112 (25%)	339 (75%)	451

If progress is not seen in this area, the CCC plans to make underrepresentation in the police department a major issue in the upcoming city council elections.

The city's affirmative action plan was welcomed by the Guardians, an organization primarily comprised of African-American police officers. The Law Enforcement Association, to which a majority of the city's white officers belong, has resolved to challenge, legally, any promotions that deviate from the past practice of hiring from the top three candidates who pass the personnel department's validated test. There have also been rumors of job slowdowns and other adverse job actions if the new plan is implemented.

There is one current opening for Police Captain. The top four candidates who passed the examination for the position are all white male officers with over 10 years in rank. The fifth candidate on the eligibility list is a bright young African-American male who had been promoted to Police Lieutenant less than two years ago.

∽○∽

INSTRUCTIONS AND QUESTIONS

You are a staff advisor to Karen Burchfield. She has asked you to outline the pros and cons of hiring the minority candidate and to make a recommendation as to what action should be taken.

32

Reasonable Accommodation

David Milligan is chief of human resources for the library system at a large, state-supported university. He is proud of the system's track record of hiring conscientious professional librarians, and likes to point out that library employees have one of the lowest absentee rates in the university.

Six months ago, however, Milligan found himself confronted by a problem that he hadn't faced before. A young librarian, Jeff Keltner, had been employed only six months when he began having emotional problems. For weeks he'd be filled with extraordinary energy, taking on extra duties and working overtime, then he'd abruptly call in sick for several days. Upon returning to work, Keltner could barely accomplish the most simple tasks. He seemed especially reluctant to have contact with the public, preferring to remain in his office during most of the workday.

It was during one of these periods that Keltner's supervisor, Dianne Moore, persuaded him to see a staff psychiatrist at the university medical center. The doctor diagnosed Keltner's condition as manic-depressive, and prescribed lithium. The drug alleviated the manic side of Keltner's moodswings, but he still suffered from periodic depressions. Antidepressants provided only partial relief, and during these periods, Keltner was often absent from work or unable to do his job effectively because he couldn't concentrate.

The situation reached a critical stage five months after Keltner's original diagnosis. Several of Keltner's co-workers began complaining that they were having to take up the slack for Keltner during his down periods. Everything was fine, they said, when he was up. Perhaps he wasn't as energetic as before, but he was still a very capable librarian when he wasn't depressed. But when he was down, Keltner often behaved unprofessionally: He stayed in his office as much as possible, and when pressed to work on the reference desk, he often became irritable and snapped at other librarians or even at patrons. His supervisor told Milligan that the other librarians were growing tired of having to calm angry students who'd had an encounter with Keltner.

Milligan finally decided to have a talk with Keltner to get some idea of his condition. He was determined to work with Keltner in any way possible to keep him on the job. But Milligan also felt an obligation to his staff in the reference section, whose morale seemed to decline every time Keltner went through one of these periods.

Milligan met with Keltner late on a Monday afternoon.

"Jeff," Milligan began, "Dianne tells me that you're still having some trouble getting your moods evened out. Seems that it's causing some problems: Some of the patrons have been getting angry with you. Now, I know you've had a rough six months, and I don't want to upset you, but what can we do to help you through these rough spots?"

"I don't know. I'm taking another drug for the depression," Keltner said, "but I just started on it a week ago, and the doctor says it takes a couple of weeks or more for it to work. And even then there's no guarantee. I don't know what I'm going to do if this one doesn't help. This is the fourth one I've tried in six months. I got a little relief from some of the others, but not enough."

"Well, what do you suggest we do in the meantime, Jeff?" Milligan asked. "Would you accept reassignment to cataloging? That way, you wouldn't have to work with the public."

"I don't have much cataloging experience," Keltner said. "I've always enjoyed working with patrons, until now. And I'm a good reference librarian."

"I know," Milligan said. "But your behavior during these periods is causing problems in the reference department. If you'd accept reassignment for a time, perhaps until they find a medicine that relieves your depression, then we could bring you back to reference."

"I don't know. I don't concentrate very well when I'm depressed, and cataloging requires good concentration. I'm not sure. And anyway, won't the people up in cataloging kind of resent me bringing my problems up there? They know about my illness, too; it's all over the library."

"Well, I think it's the best course of action right now to put you up there for three months or so and see how it works out," Milligan said. "Are you amenable to that? Take a few days and think it over, but I'd really like to see you consider it."

⋙०⋘

INSTRUCTIONS AND QUESTIONS

1. Is Milligan's offer of reassignment a reasonable accommodation of Keltner's disability? If Keltner accepts, how will it affect his career?

2. Does Keltner have a responsibility to the university to accept reassignment, considering his occasional inability to do his job effectively?

3. Design an alternative scenario for the capstone meeting between Milligan and Keltner.

4. Does Keltner have recourse under the Americans with Disabilities Act (ADA) to prevent Milligan from reassigning him to a job that he is reluctant to perform and isn't particularly qualified for?

5. Do you consider Keltner's condition a disability?

33

A Subordinate's Homophobia

In mid-June, Jack Richards was offered a position as the Research Co-ordinator for the Personnel Survey Research Center (PSRC), a relatively small unit that exists within the personnel division of a large federal agency. While PSRC primarily supports the agency's personnel and training functions through the collection of accurate, timely, and reliable information, it also contracts with other state and federal agencies to conduct survey research. In addition, the unit maintains an archive of manpower, personnel, and training data bases for the agency. The PSRC typically runs concurrently four to five large projects. Most of the projects involve individually addressed, multistage mailings, which are followed up by a series of interviews or focus groups.

Jack had just completed his graduate training, with a doctorate in social psychology and a special emphasis in program evaluation, and he quickly accepted the offer as PSRC Research Coordinator, working directly below the two PSRC directors, Drs. Ed Fagan and Melanie Jackson. The directors serve as the primary contact with contracting parties. They determine what information is needed and sketch out the project's parameters. The Research Coordinator assists with the planning process and is responsible for assigning staff to the project, creating an internal time line for completion, and overseeing all project activities. The PSRC's staff includes nine project assistants, two administrative assistants, and approximately 20 part-time interviewers.

Jack assumed the role of Research Coordinator nearly three months after his predecessor, Stephanie Miller, had resigned. During the interim, Melanie and Ed had been managing the activities of the staff, largely through the two administrative assistants. Jack found that there had been numerous problems with projects over the past year. One survey containing numerous typos and lacking several key items was mailed to over 3,000 participants, and the mistakes did not surface until several hundred completed questionnaires were returned. Other projects were badly behind schedule. In some cases, the data entry had never been scheduled with the outside contractor, while in others the interviews had not been completed. Melanie and Ed were both frustrated by the problems, and it was clear that the morale of the staff was suffering. The project assistants were particularly demoralized and seemed to be fatalistic in their expectation that mistakes would occur.

During the first few months, Jack worked hard to improve the PSRC's performance. As he became involved in the ongoing projects, Jack worked closely with the project associates to identify and solve problems. In most cases, he discussed problematic issues with a selected group of staff members and would elicit their input. Once an action plan was decided upon, it was the group's responsibility to implement the solution. During the weekly staff meetings with Melanie and Ed, Jack would ask the group members to describe the problem and explain the corrective steps that had been taken. He often followed the group's report with a comment on how quickly the problem had been resolved, and he typically emphasized the contribution of each group member.

After six months, the situation had improved greatly. All of the major projects were back on schedule and many of the past problems had been corrected. The staff morale had noticeably improved and, in many ways, the project associates had begun to work as a team. They frequently would identify potential difficulties before they occurred and would come to Jack with an action plan in hand.

During a staff meeting in early December, the annual holiday party was discussed. There was a good amount of interest among the staff, and several people expressed a desire to help. Jack agreed to host the party. Although he was somewhat apprehensive, he realized that this was a chance to be more open with his co-workers. Jack felt that though he had established a good working relationship with each of the staff members, he was still somewhat distant from them. While the staff was very friendly, he rarely socialized with them outside the office or joined in conversations about things other than work.

Jack suspected that most of the project staff already realized that he was gay. He had not hidden his sexuality during the application process and had never tried to pass as heterosexual. However, because he avoided any mention of his personal life at work, the subject never came up.

Jack guessed that the staff members were probably unsure about how to raise the topic and were waiting for him to make the first move.

The party was a great success. With the exception of Ed and his wife, everyone attended. Jack introduced his partner, John, to each guest as he or she arrived. John was quickly accepted into the group and was involved in conversation throughout the evening. As a result, Jack felt he could be much more open at work. He began mentioning John by name, would occasionally discuss their weekend plans with staff members, and even put a picture of John on his desk. The staff also seemed more comfortable. They frequently asked about John and would always invite John to attend social events.

In February, Melanie and Ed hired a new project associate, Robert Eccles. Robert had just completed his master's degree and had a strong academic background. He quickly became involved in several ongoing projects and seemed to get along with most of the staff. Though friendly, he seemed to prefer to work individually.

Although Robert was a hard worker, he had little experience with applied research and made a number of minor mistakes. The mistakes frequently occurred when he neglected to check details or failed to consult with other members of the team. In dealing with these problems, Jack noticed a certain uneasiness in Robert. He always seemed to rush through conversations with Jack and avoided looking him in the eye. In addition, Robert seemed reluctant to work through problems with Jack in a group context; Robert would neither address Jack, nor respond directly to any of Jack's comments.

As time passed, Robert increasingly ignored Jack's role in the PSRC. Rather than bringing issues to Jack, he began to raise them during staff meetings. His comments sometimes reflected poorly on one or more of the other project associates. Other comments suggested that he did not trust Jack's judgments in important decisions. In addition, Robert began to request meetings with Melanie and Ed to handle problems. While Melanie resisted these requests, Ed met with Robert whenever asked. Robert's relationship with the other project associates also seemed to worsen over time. Jack wondered if this was a result of Robert's behavior during the staff meetings or if there was more to it.

Jack decided that he needed to address the situation and arranged a meeting with Robert. He began the meeting by praising Robert's efforts and commenting that he was making an excellent contribution. He then suggested that Robert should bring problems and concerns to him first. Jack explained that, in most cases, problems could be solved by working with the other associates, and that, in the context of the staff meetings, it was better to explain how a problem was handled rather than just to present a problem.

Robert was clearly uneasy during the meeting. He never looked directly at Jack and seemed eager to end the conversation. He nodded his head each time Jack made a suggestion and would simply say, "Okay." Two days later, Jack overheard Robert talking with someone on the phone. At one point, Robert said, "God, you know Jack's a faggot. I just can't take him seriously."

∽∾o∾∾

INSTRUCTIONS AND QUESTIONS

1. Assume the role of Jack. How would you proceed at this point? Would you confront Robert about his homophobia?
2. As Jack, what risks do you foresee for yourself and the PSRC in confronting Robert about his behavior? What risks are associated with not confronting him?
3. Assume the role of Melanie Jackson. You are aware of the ineffectual working relationship between Jack and Robert. What do you do?

PART SIX

Policies and Procedures

		Page
34.	A Matter of Evaluation	169
35.	Annual Daffodil Festival	172
36.	Metropolitan Emergency Medical Services	174
37.	Of Bounded Cooperation	179
38.	The *Challenger* Shuttle Disaster	184
39.	The Gesture That Went Awry	189

34

A Matter of Evaluation

The program evaluation section of a state rehabilitation agency did not enjoy a particularly good reputation as a result of—in the opinion of many—the general incompetence of its section chief. Thus, when Buddy Kraft, an ambitious district supervisor, heard that the chief had taken a transfer to another agency, he saw the chance both to gain notice for his ability and to transfer to the central office, where the "action" is. Consequently, he put in a request to transfer into the vacant position.

Buddy was elated to hear that his request had been approved and that the agency would foot his moving bill to the state capital, some $2,000 in expenses. Upon taking over his duties, however, he soon learned that the proverbial grass was not as green as he had anticipated.

The major criticism of the evaluation section under the former chief had been that their reports were too esoteric and, though they might show technical competency and high validity from the point of view of a research analyst, the reports were not fully responsive to the needs of the field staff. Also, it usually took many revisions and some months to produce them, thereby limiting the usefulness they might have had.

Buddy has assumed that, with his field experience, plus his academic training in program evaluation (via night classes), he would be able to provide reports that were both rigorously carried out and geared to the needs of field staff. Unfortunately, there was a factor in the equation that he had overlooked.

The Division Administrator, Dr. Paul Von Stupp, is a nationally known figure in the area of research and statistics and is Buddy's immediate supervisor. He takes great pride in the Research and Statistics

Unit, of which program evaluation is a section, and in the precise methodology that it employs. He requires that program evaluation follow scientific procedure in evaluating district offices, considering only those variables predetermined to be significant.

The trouble began at the first field evaluation. The District Administrator requested that the evaluators look into a morale problem concerning the clerical staff. The Administrator confided to Buddy that he had not been able to get a handle on it, that it was beginning to adversely affect client services, and that perhaps an outside evaluation team would be able to elicit the clerks' confidence and discover the cause. Buddy, seizing upon the opportunity to improve the unit's tarnished credibility, phoned Dr. Von Stupp for authority to broaden the scope of the evaluation to include interviews with clerical staff. Buddy's request was denied and he was admonished for attempting to include "extraneous variables" in the report. Matters became even worse when his superior required five revisions of the report because of such trivial concerns as the placing of tables, and references to obscure authorities in the literature.

Publication of the report was delayed some four months, and in final form it looked very much like the unit's typical and much-maligned product. In the process of developing the report, Buddy had frequent differences with the Division Administrator over the revisions, and is now at odds with him—hardly a positive situation in view of his upcoming probationary performance review.

Buddy is now in a pickle. It appears that his boss's rigidity will not allow him to carry out the type of evaluation that the Division of Field Operations would like, even though, as he has heard, the agency director is becoming dissatisfied with his section's performance. Also, continual attempts to get Von Stupp to change his ways may well jeopardize a satisfactory probationary report and future promotions. Other section staff members, dissatisfied with what they consider to be irrelevant evaluations, have begun transferring out, increasing the turnover rate.

Buddy knows that, if he transfers to another unit, it may make him appear uncommitted and an opportunist. If he returns to his old job, he will owe the state the original moving cost and will have to bear the expense of the move back himself. Going around the chain of command may also get him into trouble, and staying where he is may be detrimental to his career, since many in the organization will associate him with the section's poor performance? What to do?

INSTRUCTIONS AND QUESTIONS

You are Buddy, and you ponder six questions.

1. What forces can you line up to your advantage?
2. Which forces seem in opposition?
3. Are there alliances you can form?
4. What are the risks?
5. Should you assume the Division Administrator to be a lost cause?
6. Should you consider a change in agencies?

35

Annual Daffodil Festival

The Daffodil Festival, a traditional celebration of the arrival of spring, has been held for the past 25 years in the town of Mountain Ridge, known for the colorful daffodils that bloom throughout the historic state park there. Over 60,000 people visited the park during last year's celebration.

One of the features of the festival is a handmade craft show that includes woodwork, pottery, cloth crafts, tinware, ceramics, baskets, quilts, leather craft, and stained glass. Unfortunately, in recent years the park administration has been faced with many more craft vendor applicants than can be reasonably accommodated in the old historic state park. As a result, Park Superintendent Barry Ford and his staff decided to limit the number of vendors allowed to participate this year. In all, 304 applications were received for 185 spaces, and another 60 applications that arrived after the deadline were sent back unopened.

To reduce the applicants to 185, Ford chose a six-member jury of park employees to examine unidentified photographs of the crafts submitted by applicants. Each jury member ranked all entries on a 1-to-5 scale, and those with the highest combined scores were selected.

Jake Robinson, director of the state's Parks and Tourism Department, considered Ford's selection process impartial. But the new method angered at least one craft vendor, Denver Gorton, who was excluded from this year's fair. Gorton, who is retired, said that his supplemental income was limited because he wasn't chosen. "The spring Daffodil Festival is my biggest show of the year," he said. "I make several thousand dollars there." He also charged that many of the selected vendors sold crafts that were inferior to his.

Gorton, a lifelong Republican in a traditionally Democratic state, wrote a long, rambling letter to the Governor, accusing the Park Superintendent of unethical behavior, and demanding an investigation of the selection process. He sent copies to his state representatives, the local media, and the state Director of Parks and Tourism. The single statewide newspaper followed with a series of articles describing the controversy, and noted that none of the government officials who received the letter had yet bothered to reply to Gorton.

∽о∾

INSTRUCTIONS AND QUESTIONS

1. Is there an unbiased way of selecting applicants that still ensures that high-quality crafts are sold at the festival?

2. Should Superintendent Ford consider changing the park's vendor selection policy in light of Gorton's complaint, or should he maintain the policy for a couple of years to see if it is effective?

3. How should Ford deal with the political pressure that could result from his decision?

4. Does Gorton have a legitimate grievance against the way the Parks and Tourism Department handled the shortage of space? Is the Superintendent within his rights to limit the number who participate, or should the park administration, as part of a public agency, make an effort to accommodate all vendors?

36

Metropolitan Emergency Medical Services

Every year approximately 11,000 deaths occur in the Sunnyside metro area. Of these, 6,000 people die from what are termed sudden death—acute, sudden illness or injury. Authorities estimate that more than 500 lives can be saved each year through the use of a coordinated emergency medical service system, which would maintain a minimal standard of service for the entire region.

The Metropolitan Emergency Medical Services (MEMS), a nonprofit agency, became operational approximately 10 years ago. To try to minimize the possibility of sudden death from illness or injury, a system was developed that would enable MEMS to dispatch the closest ambulance (public or private) to the scene of an emergency. MEMS provides a single seven-digit phone number for persons to report emergencies throughout the 17-county metropolitan area. The MEMS system, though technically well designed and staffed with qualified personnel, has no power to coerce participation and hence cannot authoritatively allocate the emergency calls that the ambulance firms depend on for their livelihood.

The MEMS system divides the 17-county metro area into eight disaster zones. The central disaster zone is at the core, and each of the other zones fans out from the central zone and is bisected by a major transportation artery. Within each disaster zone, a physician is assigned as the Zone On-Site Medical Director. In the event of a disaster, the Zone Director will assume control upon arrival at the scene. Each Zone Director is familiar with the specific medical resources and geography of his or her area and has complete knowledge of the MEMS communications system.

The MEMS communications system provides the Zone Director with a tremendous inventory of medical expertise. The MEMS center is a patchwork of communications equipment. The center provides for multiple communications modes—radio to telephone, radio to radio, telephone to radio, and telephone to telephone. These capabilities enable the MEMS coordinator to "patch" a physician to the regional Poison Control Center, or to patch an emergency medical technician with a portable radio through to a physician at an emergency room or even at home. The MEMS system also enables area ambulances to talk directly with each other during a disaster. The MEMS system covers approximately 3,000 square miles, and its first major accomplishment was to reduce some 2,000 emergency telephone numbers to one.

The MEMS system received an initial grant of $400,000 from the Robert Wood Johnson Foundation. This grant, however, does not fully provide for the needs of the system, and through last year, MEMS received practically all its funding from a 15-cent-per-capita donation from five counties. It also received a federal Health and Human Services grant totalling $250,000, as well as other private grants in excess of $50,000.

A major budgetary setback occurred during the last fiscal year. Because some counties became unwilling to help meet MEMS' financial needs, its budget was reduced by $133,000, nearly one-fourth of its operating budget.

The financial setback has multiple causes, which some details will help explain. MEMS uses a redundant computer system especially designed for its requirements. The computer automatically identifies the three nearest ambulances, shows their locations on a street map, and then coordinates and estimates the time of arrival for each ambulance. It also identifies the ambulance as either an advanced or a basic life-support unit. The MEMS communicator then selects the appropriate unit, or two if an advanced unit is required but is more than six minutes away. This information is transferred through video readouts to the ambulance dispatcher. The dispatcher then contacts the ambulance.

The location and status of vehicles, whether stationary or en route, are maintained simultaneously, and their position is updated automatically every 30 seconds from the last-known position.

Participation in MEMS is voluntary on the part of the ambulance firms. These firms include both public and private ambulance services. Publicly supported ambulance services were willing to participate freely in MEMS, but private operators began to express increasing reservations. Private operators at first were enthusiastic about MEMS, but

they increasingly came to believe that promises concerning the distribution of emergency calls had not been kept. Complex interests were at
issue.

Fifteen ambulance services, public and private, participate in MEMS.
There are 56 life-support units within the MEMS operation. Of these
units, 20 belong to Gorham Memorial Hospital (public), and 18 belong to
Sunnyside Ambulance Service (private). Two counties subsidize private
firms in their areas, but the remaining counties do not. Some of the companies need additional business badly, others do not; some receive funds
to carry indigent patients, others do not.

Some of the smaller companies say they are not getting enough calls
to remain fiscally solvent. The small companies have two to four ambulances, and contend that MEMS has reduced the number of calls they
receive. This stems from the fact that the two largest ambulance
providers—Gorham and Sunnyside—have allowed MEMS to place
some of their vehicles at strategic locations. Often, this positions a competing ambulance firm in the areas where the smaller firms once operated exclusively. MEMS has succeeded in providing a more efficient use
of vehicles, but as a by-product has placed some of the smaller firms in
a fiscally precarious situation. More than the immediate self-interest of
the smaller firms may be involved. Their failure might decrease the
number of ambulances and trained personnel. The threatened companies contend that this would ultimately serve to lower the quality of
emergency medical services through the entire system.

The dilemmas are clear to all observers. If MEMS provides adequate
emergency medical coverage to the citizens in the 17 counties it serves,
it may (and probably will) eventually force some of the providers of
these services into positions that are not economically viable. But if
MEMS does not shift some of the existing capacity, needless deaths will
probably occur. The small ambulance firms, though their participation is
voluntary, cannot afford to pull out. As the public becomes more aware
of the MEMS emergency number, more and more citizens will rely sole-
ly on it. In fact, the fire and police departments of all 17 counties already use MEMS exclusively when requesting ambulance assistance.
Thus, no small firm can afford to drop out of the program.

The larger providers have various stakes in MEMS. The Gorham ambulance service receives funds from county and federal governments,
and therefore does not look to its ambulance service to generate income.
Moreover, except for the drivers, Gorham ambulances are staffed with
interns and student nurses, who receive little or no pay. Sunnyside Ambulance Service is in a different position. The only funds it receives are
those earned from ambulance calls, and competition from Gorham via

MEMS has its costs. But Sunnyside benefits from the fact that its once-underutilized capacity is now placed in a more productive location.

In sum, MEMS decisions are of extreme economic concern to the majority of the firms that participate in the program. More than the life-and-death calls that allow for the care and aid of citizens, MEMS faces decisions that could also mean life or death to some of the private firms involved in the program.

The crunch often comes in getting firms to respond to emergency calls. MEMS cannot force any ambulance firm to go anywhere it does not wish. This means, for example, that some areas, especially those of low income, do not have adequate coverage. Some counties compensate firms for the indigent calls they receive, but other counties do not.

This situation can sometimes have tragic results. Consider one emergency call, which occurs about four o'clock on a Wednesday afternoon. Mrs. Jones is visiting from another state, and suffers an epileptic seizure. Her daughter requests an ambulance. The first MEMS call goes to a private ambulance three minutes away, which refuses the call because Mrs. Jones is in a poor section of an outlying county. The second closest ambulance, from the same firm, also refuses the call. The third and final ambulance listed on the computer readout is a small private firm. Its personnel know they are not the closest ambulance to the scene of the emergency, and ask why others did not take the call. They are told about the refusal, and respond that they already have taken their fair share of similar cases.

The MEMS dispatcher runs through a second readout to find the next three nearest ambulances, all of which are over 20 minutes away from the emergency. A Gorham ambulance is on the list, and since it is publically financed, it will respond to this call. But many minutes have elapsed since the call about Mrs. Jones came through, and it will be another 22 to 25 minutes before the Gorham ambulance can reach her.

∾o∾

INSTRUCTIONS AND QUESTIONS

As a federal official who encouraged the Johnson Foundation grant and followed it with a $250,000 federal grant to this system, you have a strong commitment to seeing it work. You believe that MEMS needs some external follow-through, but there is a limited amount of money available to grant to MEMS for this purpose—between $100,000 and $200,000. You know that the system as designed depends on voluntary participation. But you also recognize that the system itself, however effective in operation, has forever altered the ethical responsibilities and legal obligations of the various possible participants.

Presuming that you have the grant funds available to use wisely, and that MEMS is located in the state where you are reading this, spend some time in a law library exploring the relevant portions of your state codes—health and welfare, criminal (penal), government, civil (business licenses, torts), and the like—to identify the local obligations of public and private ambulance services and the powers of regional and local authorities in these matters. Prepare a brief summary of your findings.

Now develop a strategy for investing your grant funds to successfully tighten up MEMS and largely eliminate the problem of refused calls. Be as specific as you need be, including drafting statutory amendments and a strategy for assuring their adoption.

37

Of Bounded Cooperation

In the Army's criminal investigation structure, a regional office is a headquartered group that controls many small units (detachments) spread throughout a large area. The regional commander sets the policy and exercises command over these units by relying on infrequent visits, telephone calls, and written reports to evaluate the operational effectiveness of his subordinate units.

A Criminal Investigation Detachment typically consists of one commissioned officer, numerous warrant officers, and several enlisted personnel. The commissioned officer is in command. One of the warrant officers—the operations officer—assigns cases to be investigated, checks the work, and, in general, acts as the second in command.

The detachment's mission is to support the commander of the military installation at which it is located. Personnel are charged mainly with the investigation of all felonies, background investigations, and investigations into activities that may affect the image of the Department of the Army.

Dealing with criminal investigators (warrant officers) can be quite an experience. Some describe them as "prima donnas" who are hard to get along with and who lack respect for inexperienced detachment commanders. Others find them to be professional people, well trained in their work, proud of what they do, honest, and determined to respect the confidence that others place in them.

PART I: A PROBLEM

One new detachment commander, Fred Steel, came to have experiences that provided some evidence of the validity of both these contrasting images of the criminal investigators.

Like all new commanders, Fred Steel visited regional headquarters prior to assuming command of his detachment. During the briefing, he is informed by the regional commander and staff that the detachment he is to command is an outstanding unit, investigatively. But, administratively, the detachment has some weak areas.

The problem the regional commander wants resolved first is the lack of an informant file. On every prior inspection, the unit is faulted for the absence of such a file. None of the prior commanders had been able to establish one. Steel hears the message clearly. Establish the informant file and soon, or go the way of the previous detachment commanders who received lackluster efficiency reports.

The informant file is nothing more than a collection of 3" × 5" index cards listing informants' names, their locations, the type of information they can provide, and the investigators' names. These cards are turned in to the operations officer, who secures them in a safe until they are needed. Used properly, these cards provide leads that can facilitate an investigation or provide intelligence of illegal activity. Normally, they are used in the following manner: Assume that a criminal investigator is assigned to work on a case involving theft at the commissary. Should he or she conduct an open investigation, the persons involved probably would stop their activities until the investigation stopped. To plant an undercover agent in the commissary is costly and time-consuming, and it may not provide the information desired. The prudent investigator, therefore, goes to the operations officer and requests a look through the informant file—hoping to find an informant in the commissary. If one is listed, the investigator may seek to use him or her.

After reporting in, Steel takes several days to observe the detachment, meet the personnel, and become somewhat familiar with the overall operation. Only then does Steel talk with the operations officer and start laying the groundwork for future policy changes. When advised of the intended meeting, the operations officer says, "Sir, I hope you are not going to attempt to establish an informant file." Steel proceeds to give the operations officer the details of his meeting with the regional commander and its loud-and-clear stated priority. Steel does not press for action, however.

About two weeks later, Steel holds his first full office conference. Here he informs all personnel of his policies and methods of operation. Last, he mentions the informant file and states that the office will initiate one.

The investigators object, in stereo. Their major points are:

1. The informants I use are mine because I have worked to establish and cultivate them.
2. My informants will work only for me.
3. If I turn in a list of informants, their identities will no longer be confidential. I have promised my informants that only I would know who they were, and I will not go back on my word. If nothing else, if any of us reneged, pretty soon no one would have any informants.
4. If I have to turn in a list of informants, then I really don't have any.

∽०∽
INSTRUCTIONS AND QUESTIONS

Imagine you are Steel.

1. How do you evaluate these objections?
2. Can you meet your own goals and the objections at the same time?

Before reading further, it should be fun to work with Steel's dilemma a little on your own. In Part II you can read how Steel really did respond.

PART II: ONE RESOLUTION

After listening to the objections of the investigators, Steel explains how his plan would work.

Everyone will return to his or her office and think about the following:

1. Every member of the detachment is a member of a team. To ensure that the team will function properly, the members should be willing to help each other when the need arises, even if it means that one investigator will let another use his or her informants.
2. Informant names are the property of the Army, as is the other information the investigator obtains.

3. Both the regional commander and Army policy require that an informant file will be kept.

Once everyone has had sufficient time to consider these points, each investigator is to complete one or more informant cards, placing each in a separate white envelope, which is to be sealed.

Investigators are to write their name and the date on the envelope, as well as the informant's location, that is, commissary or post exchange.

Investigators then will take the envelopes to the operations officer, who will sign his or her name across the sealed flap, placing a strip of clear tape across the signature and the flap.

The envelopes, unopened, will be placed in a safe, thereby keeping the name of the informant confidential.

During the course of an investigation, should an investigator need an informant, he or she will go to the operations officer, who will check the file for an informant in the required location. If any suitable envelopes exist, the operations officer will give the inquiring investigator the name or names of those who filed the envelope(s). The two or more investigators will have to work out mutually the method of using any informant.

Envelopes will be opened only:

1. On an investigator's departure from the detachment.
2. In the event of an emergency, and under order from the detachment commander.

Finally, Steel states he is not interested in the names of any informants. He is only interested in following regulations and providing assistance to investigators in the detachment.

On that note, Steel concludes the conference and leaves without knowing how his people will react to his plan. But he does feel a little uneasy about their acceptance of it.

Over the course of the next few days, the operations officer receives envelopes from every investigator. Steel is told that the operations officer is confident that each envelope contains the required information. Initially, the informant file contained about 20 envelopes. Thirty days later there are 70 envelopes in the file.

∽ॐ∾
INSTRUCTIONS AND QUESTIONS

1. Evaluate Steel's plan. Does it accomplish his purpose and that of the regional commander?
2. Are there any vulnerable features of the plan?
3. How would you propose evaluating whether or not the file was contributing to more effective investigations?

38

The *Challenger* Shuttle Disaster

Millions of television viewers, including thousands of schoolchildren, watched in horror on the morning of January 28, 1986, as the space shuttle *Challenger* burst into flames shortly after liftoff. Over the following weeks, viewers saw the fiery flash and falling debris replayed repeatedly on television as the shuttle carrying teacher Christa McAuliffe and six astronauts disappeared in a raging fireball.

President Reagan responded quickly and appointed the Rogers Commission to investigate the disaster. The Commission issued its report by early June (U.S. Presidential Commission on the Space Shuttle *Challenger* Accident, 1986). After an intensive investigation and public testimony, most experts concurred that the immediate cause of the explosion was physical: Two O-rings designed to seal joints together on *Challenger's* right booster rocket failed. Pressures from gases inside the solid rocket booster caused it to expand. As the booster rocket expanded, its segments rotated against each other. Initially the heat that melted the O-rings and the putty surrounding them formed a temporary seal. As the shuttle accelerated, the seal broke, releasing a stream of hot gases that ignited an external liquid-fuel tank, resulting in the fatal explosion.

NASA was clearly experiencing some major organizational problems at this time. It was operating under severe resource constraints, hostile constituents, and overseers, and its "management had a propensity to contain potentially serious problems and to attempt to resolve them internally rather than communicate them forward," according to the Rogers Commission.

The Commission called the decision-making system for the shuttle program "clearly flawed." Fifteen engineers employed by Morton-Thiokol, Inc., the firm that manufactured the booster rocket, initially opposed the launch, fearing potential O-ring problems in the unusually cold Florida weather. NASA officials, however, were preoccupied with mending fences with a budget-conscious Congress and White House, both of which were being inundated with complaints from commercial and military clients about the shuttle's undependable flight schedule.

The following excerpts are taken from hearing testimony conducted by the Rogers Commission*:

CHAIRMAN ROGERS: One of our responsibilities is to attempt to determine the cause or causes of the accident. Do you want to give us your name?

MR. BOISJOLY: My name is Roger Boisjoly, and I'm in the Structures Section at Morton-Thiokol, Inc. I have been involved with these seals basically since I've come to work for Thiokol, which was some five and a half years ago. I first heard of the cold temperatures prior to launch at one o'clock on the day before the launch, and from past experience, it just concerned me terribly. Consequently, we began to question the feasibility of launching at such a low temperature.

DR. WALKER: And the O-ring was your concern?

MR. BOISJOLY: Yes. I felt we were very successful up until early evening, because it culminated in the recommendation not to fly, and that was the initial conclusion. I was quite pleased with that.

MR. BOISJOLY: I explained (during a telecon set-up with Kennedy Space Center and Marshall Space Flight Center in mid-evening, approximately 8:00 P.M.) that I was deeply concerned about launching due to the low temperature and its effect on the O-rings. George Hardy (NASA) was then asked by someone at either Kennedy Space Center or Marshall Space Flight Center what he thought. He said he was appalled at Morton-Thiokol, Inc.'s, recommendation. He was then asked if he would fly, and he said no if the contractor is recommending not to fly.

(A short discussion by various people followed. Morton-Thiokol, Inc.'s, management asked for a short, five-minute caucus off-line, and said they would get right back to them. The caucus lasted approximately 20 to 25 minutes.)

*See *Rogers Commission* report, February 16, June 10, and 17, 1986. United States Senate, Subcommittee on Science, Technology, and Space.

Morton-Thiokol, Inc.'s, management team subsequently went back on the telecon and made the recommendation to launch without any temperature restrictions.

MR. BOISJOLY: One of my colleagues that was in the meeting summed it up best. This was a meeting where the determination was to launch, and it was up to us to prove beyond a shadow of a doubt that it was not safe to do so. This is a total reverse to what the position usually is in a preflight conversation or a flight readiness review. It is usually exactly opposite that. I left the room feeling badly defeated, but felt I did all I could short of being fired. I personally felt that management was under a lot of pressure to launch and that they made a very tough decision, and I didn't agree with it.

DR. WALKER: Do you know the source of the pressure on management that you alluded to?

MR. BOISJOLY: Well, the comments made over the (telecon) net are what I felt, I can't speak for them, but I felt it—I felt the tone of the meeting exactly as I summed up, that we were being put in a position to prove that we should not launch rather than being put in the position to prove that we had enough data to launch.

CHAIRMAN ROGERS: Thank you very much. Mr. Lund do you want to give your name and position?

MR. LUND: My name is Robert Lund, and I am Vice-President of Engineering at Morton-Thiokol, Inc.

CHAIRMAN ROGERS: How do you explain the fact that you seemed to change your mind when you took off your engineering hat and put on your management hat?

MR. LUND: Our original recommendation, of course, was not to launch.

DR. WALKER: Well, I understood that, but your final recommendation was to launch.

MR. LUND: Okay, What we need to do, then, is go through that rationale.

MR. WALKER: So you are going to answer my question, then, at the end of this discussion, hopefully?

MR. LUND: If you want me to go through it now, I would be glad to do that.

CHAIRMAN ROGERS: Well, I think we have heard your explanation. I think the problem we are having, is that it is not convincing. I mean, let me, if you don't mind, I assume you have great confidence in your engineers Boisjoly and Thompson and the others, and they are probably as well qualified as anyone in the country in dealing with these problems of O-rings and seals and so forth, is that right?

MR. LUND: Yes.

CHAIRMAN ROGERS: And you had a long discussion in the telecon, and you decided, all of you, I understand, that for safety reasons, you would oppose the launch. Thereafter, NASA, in one way or another, made it clear that they were displeased with that recommendation, and I assume that you knew when you made the recommendation that it was going to determine whether the shuttle would be launched or not because NASA had indicated to you that they would not fly unless they had a written report from Thiokol saying you approved the launch.

MR. LUND: I didn't know NASA would accept that.

CHAIRMAN ROGERS: You didn't know that?

MR. LUND: No.

CHAIRMAN ROGERS: Well, you must have known your recommendation was very important. You knew that if you voted against the launch it would not have been launched, didn't you?

MR. LUND: Well, we had voted prior to it, and they didn't accept it, so I couldn't forecast what NASA would do.

CHAIRMAN ROGERS: But you know that that was the reason they asked you to reconsider. Isn't that why you had the five-minute recess?

MR. LUND: That's a fair statement, yes.

CHAIRMAN ROGERS: Now, knowing that, and knowing that the safety of the crew was involved, and knowing your own people, the engineers that you respected, were still against the launch, what was it that occurred in your mind that satisfied you to say okay, let's take a chance?

MR. LUND: Well, I didn't say let's take a chance. However, I did feel that there was some rationale that allowed us to go ahead.

CHAIRMAN LUND: Well, maybe that isn't fair. Then what was it that occurred in your mind that caused you to be willing to change your mind?

〜o〜

INSTRUCTIONS AND QUESTIONS

1. What can organizations, in general, do to make decisions when there is uncertainty about, or conflict over, cause-and-effect relationships (that is, over the means to particular ends)?

2. How should an organization proceed when its goals are ambiguous or in conflict?

3. How should an organization go about prioritizing goals or making acceptable trade-offs?

4. Differing diagnoses of organizational problems leading up to the *Challenger* disaster will correspondingly produce different prescriptions. What political reasons may have influenced Mr. Lund to change his mind and decide to go ahead and launch the shuttle?

39

The Gesture That Went Awry

Cynthia Rynick had worked for Ringold City for approximately 10 months. During her initial job interview, and prior to accepting her position with the city, she told her soon-to-be-boss and the Personnel Director that she was planning to get married the following year in October. Also, she was requesting one week off "with pay" for her honeymoon. Her request was acknowledged by both of the interviewers and she was given a "verbal" promise of time off with pay.

After a couple of months, Cynthia reminds her immediate supervisor that she is getting married in October and asks if she could use one of her two vacation weeks in advance for her honeymoon. In the past, supervisors would routinely grant their employees advanced time off and charge it against their vacation time earned for the following year. Cynthia reasoned that she would have earned the two weeks of vacation time by January.

Cynthia's immediate supervisor, after checking with the Personnel Director and receiving approval, informs her that there should be no problem in granting her request. Six weeks pass, and Cynthia approaches her supervisor once again in an attempt to receive some type of written approval of her request. Cynthia's supervisor is dismayed to find out that the Personnel Director is now opposed to the request for fear of setting a precedent for other employees who might make similar requests. The Personnel Director remembers the havoc that resulted in the past when similar requests were granted on a routine basis.

However, during an informal luncheon with the City Manager and Mayor, Cynthia makes the comment that her request for advancement on her vacation time has been denied by the Personnel Director. The

Mayor and City Manager are "shocked" that this model employee is not being given the adequate respect they feel she deserves, so they subsequently promise her that she will receive the week off with pay and she can use next year's vacation time in advance. In addition to the verbal promise made at lunch, the City Manager sends Cynthia a memo that indicates his desire for her to receive the week off with pay.

Cynthia proceeds with her honeymoon plans but is terribly shocked to find out that the Personnel Department has denied her vacation request despite the verbal and written promises made by the City Manager and the Mayor. Cynthia soon learns that a formal grievance was filed by the union against the City Manager. According to the contract between the union and Ringold City, "each permanent full-time employee who has at least one (1) year's seniority shall, after the completion of his or her first and subsequent full year of service in permanent full-time status, be entitled to an annual two-week vacation with pay during the next ensuing year."

Cynthia knows that exceptions to the contract have been granted in the past, but now there is some animosity between the Personnel Director and the City Manager. In fact, the Personnel Director informed the union president of the pending agreement between the City Manager and Cynthia Rynick. The Personnel Director knew that the union would be forced to file a grievance about the contract violation and, furthermore, a black employee was denied a similar request a few months ago. How would it look to grant special privileges to certain employees and not others? The city could have a discrimination suit on its hands. Cynthia also learns that the Personnel Director had applied for the City Manager's job when it opened up two years ago but did not get it.

∽०∾

INSTRUCTIONS AND QUESTIONS

1. If you were Cynthia, what would you do?
2. If you were the City Manager, what would you do?

PART SEVEN

Supervisory Problems

		Page
40.	An Office Romance	193
41.	Carl the Ripper	197
42.	Conflicts on the Human Services Coordination Team	200
43.	The Making of a Corrections Officer	207
44.	Distributing County Property Without Consent	213
45.	Easing Toward Change in Urbania's Finance Department	215
46.	"Keep a Two-by-Four Behind Your Desk"	220
47.	"Stop Having Birthdays!"	224
48.	One Supervisor's Analysis	229

40

An Office Romance

You, John French, are the deputy director of a state Department of Housing and Community Development. Donald Chicago is one of the division heads who reports to you. Donald has never been your favorite division head; he does his job well enough, but nobody has ever seen him stay after five. Donald has been a quiet employee and does not socialize much. In fact, only a few of his colleagues have more than a passing acquaintance with him.

Things changed sharply for the worse about a year ago when Ginny Holden came on board after making a big splash in her first job out of graduate school. Ginny and Donald soon became a "hot item," so much so that you asked Donald to meet with you during December of last year. You told him of the rumors that you had heard. "Look Don," you told him then, "I believe that your personal life is *your* personal life. I try to stay out of these matters unless they affect the office. But you and Ginny Holden are sure making things hard for me."

In prepping for that meeting, you consulted Chicago's file, and it provided many details that you augment with discreet inquiries here and there. Donald Chicago had been with Housing and Community Development for eight years—with housing assistance all that time, beginning as a branch chief in construction assistance and moving up deliberately. Now he has over 75 people reporting to him in several sections—construction assistance, rent supplements, rent subsidies, technical assistance in housing management, and the like. As far as anyone knows, Donald has a happy family life. He had pictures on his desk, showed up dutifully at office parties with his wife, and talked about her with affection. He lives in a nice neighborhood in the city rather than in the suburbs and sends his three children to public schools. He is 41 years old, holds an honorable discharge from the Air Force, attended the state university after military service, and has 16 years of progressively responsible community-development experience—eight years in the department and, before that, eight years in two city governments.

Nobody had spoken ill of Donald until very recently. In fact, nobody had spoken about him much at all. The fact that he had no friends or enemies may have contributed to his steady rise in the agency. His is a department occasionally plagued by interpersonal rivalries among people on the way up.

Getting information about Ginny Holden was no problem. She is among everyone's favorite topics. She had been abroad for only a year, and already controversy engulfed her. She is bright, no denying that. She had come to the technical-assistance program from the state's second-largest city, which was in the western part of the state. There she had apparently energized a languishing housing-for-the-elderly program. The community-development director, the area's senior citizens, and the mayor had all written of her in glowing terms. She had made quite a splash for someone right out of graduate school.

Her work in your agency reveals no shortcomings either. The first reports on her were very positive. Only after Ginny and Don got involved did any complaints surface. At first, you attributed the complaints to jealousy and rivalry. Capable, ambitious people usually occasion some hostility, especially if they are women. Even with all the gossip, no one dares assert that Ginny's work is other than the best in the division. The local officials love her too. It is Don who has the problem. And you, the deputy director.

Of course, Ginny might have been more discreet about it. When the affair began, about six months ago, Ginny would tell her co-workers: "Don't tell anybody else, but Don and I are, well, you know. I just never thought anything like this would happen to me!" At least that's what you learned through the grapevine. Having held Don's job yourself once, you have more than enough friends in the right places.

You told Donald during your December meeting last year what you heard. Donald said that he could not stop her talking, if she wanted to talk. Besides, he did not mind some attention for once in his life. You tried to warn Donald that he has a lot to lose, far more that Ginny, who is more than 15 years his junior.

Gossip is not the problem for John French. The department has its share of "closed minds" or "good family people"—take your pick—particularly among the office staff. And they often get quietly offended. As long as the matter stays in house, that resentment is not a major factor.

But you begin to get an inquiry or two from the capitol building about Don's "fun and games." You guess that the office network has begun to latch on to this story.

The developing grapevine causes you concern. There could be some bad press for the department if the papers want to make something of this. Since the local communities compete vigorously for the department's attention, you want to be on top of anything that might inspire charges of favoritism. Could Donald be blackmailed? The department has its enemies, too. Some politicians and some newspapers have never accepted the government's role in housing. Given the clientele and the nature of the programs, occasional scandal seems practically inevitable, but you see no sense in courting it! Donald has no constituency to defend him, either. He is just a guy doing a job—no politics, no ethnic loyalty, no programmatic cause. Your 41-year-old division chief, having one hell of an affair, has a clean if not distinguished record up to now.

The first specific item that worries you is a complaint that Ginny Holden is getting the best fieldwork assignments. She seems to get out into the state capital often. Ginny has even traveled to Washington twice, once with Don, as well as to the Housing and Urban Development (HUD) regional office several times. Don says she is the most capable person to do the work he needed done. Others feel he could spread the travel around in the interest of office morale, with no loss to divisional effectiveness. There is a lot of grumbling when Ginny gets a small promotion and reclassification after only five months on the job. True, she was not working directly for Don, and you are not sure that Bill Hayes—her immediate supervisor—even knew about their affair. Hayes is not the most observant soul and is not cognizant about the situation.

Thus, the grapevine continues. Your agency is full of reasonably cosmopolitan people on the professional staff. There is a women's caucus, which grumbles about bad Ginny "sleeping her way to the top" while they also grumble about poor Ginny's exploitation. Similar sentiments can be heard among the men, though the language has a gamier quality. The small gay caucus has even approached you quietly about Ginny and her friend.

Now, in February, you grow increasingly convinced that another meeting with Don is necessary, and you have to take a far harder line. Things have become much worse since you last discussed Donald's personal life with him. What especially provokes this meeting is Don's work itself. You did not mind when he grew a moustache or took an occasional afternoon off. But now you hear that he does not return phone calls. A couple of quarterly reports have come in several days late. Semi-annual personnel evaluations from the division seem behind schedule. You have received two calls in the past two weeks from local community-development directors you know, each inquiring about the delays in Don's division.

You begin to wish that Don would simply walk in and say that he's decided to take a year off to study planning in southern France. You are not that lucky. Instead, Donald Chicago will walk into your office in five minutes with his usual blank smile and ask sincerely what he can do for you today.

∽◦∾

INSTRUCTIONS AND QUESTIONS

You are deputy director John French.

1. What are the options facing you at this point? Presume that you must contend with a normal civil-service system.

2. Research the case law in this matter. Can Donald Chicago be fired if he "offends" agency or community standards?

3. This kind of meeting will not be enjoyable for any of the participants. Can you present some psychological or group-dynamics theories that illuminate some of the reasons for discomfort in ways that will help you, as deputy director, keep attention on resolving this matter with the least harm to Donald and the department?

4. Is there something more general at issue here?

41

Carl the Ripper

PART ONE

In June, Laurie Martin was hired as an administrative assistant by the area office of a federal agency on the West Coast. Laurie was a college graduate and was certified to teach high school, but she had been unable to secure employment in her profession. She had worked nearly two years as a clerk-typist for a large private corporation located in the suburb where she lives. Even though the higher salary of the new job would barely cover commuting costs, Laurie willingly changed jobs because of the promise of advancement.

Rose Wong is the supervisor of Laurie's unit. She has worked within the agency for more than 20 years and has a reputation for efficiency and accuracy. She oversees Laurie's work and that of four court reporters. Rose liked Laurie when she interviewed her and recommended that assistant director Wes Jennings hire Laurie.

When Laurie started working for Rose, she was overwhelmed by Rose's stringent requirements. If the work was not perfect, it was rejected and Laurie had to do it again. Rose's tactics frustrated Laurie, but she was determined to win the approval of her supervisor.

After a month of being frustrated by Rose, Laurie went to Wes and asked if there were vacancies in any less regimented unit of the agency. Wes informed her that the only vacancy was a position in a pay grade lower than Laurie's. Since Laurie's education and experience qualified her to be three pay grades higher than she was, she decided against dropping further down the pay scale in the hope of eventually going upward.

Laurie continued to work for Rose, trying to convince herself that Rose's actions were part of an initiation into the agency. It seemed to her, though, that Rose wanted her to quit. For example, Laurie remembered her embarrassment when Rose required her to announce when she had to use the ladies' room, and then told her that she had taken too long when she returned.

One day during the first week of August, Rose has a family emergency and is out of the office for two days. Wanda Blake, the assistant supervisor, takes over the duties. The employees are more relaxed and friendly during these two days, and Laurie finally becomes acquainted with her co-workers. They tell her that they also had undergone similar, although not as harsh, initiations. They also assure Laurie that once Rose accepts someone she is thenceforth fiercely loyal.

When Rose returns, she begins praising Laurie's work. About a week later, Rose asks Laurie if she would be interested in taking on additional duties, of course at a higher pay grade. She says she is pleased with Laurie's work and feels that she is capable of meeting this new challenge. Laurie is stunned but manages to respond affirmatively to Rose's offer.

Laurie is very excited about this new promotion until she learns that Carl Johnson will train her. She does not like Carl. In their few previous meetings, he continually bragged about his sexual conquests and announced early that she would be his next one. Laurie is not interested in him, period. Carl is a married man with six children; he is 20 years older than Laurie; and besides, she already has a steady boyfriend.

When Carl learns that he is to be Laurie's instructor, he tells her that his recommendation about her training will depend on her sexual performance. He emphasizes his statement by fondling her breasts, then quickly leaves the room before she can say or do anything.

The next afternoon, Carl and Laurie are alone in the office for a few minutes. Carl asks Laurie to come over to his desk. While she is standing by his desk, he puts his hand up her dress. Laurie grabs his hand and slams it down on the desk, telling him to keep his hands to himself.

Carl grows white with rage. "If you ever resist me again," he warns Laurie, "I'll throw you on the floor and plank you right here."

༄

INSTRUCTIONS AND QUESTIONS

You are Laurie. What do you do?

PART TWO

Laurie goes to Wes Jennings's office and resigns from her position. Wes is shocked by Laurie's sudden announcement and tells her so. He presses her for details, and she finally tells him about the threats she received from a male co-worker, whom she does not identify. Laurie says only that the man threatened physical violence.

Wes tells her again how sorry he is to have her leave. He asks her if she would reconsider, and she declines. He then says:

"You know, Laurie, when I hired you, Rose bet me a lunch at Kuoh Wah's Restaurant that you wouldn't last six months in her unit. She has been so pleased with your progress, however, that she called off the bet and recommended that you be promoted to a higher position. I know she'll be disappointed when she learns that you have decided to leave us. I wish you would discuss your decision with her."

Laurie does not commit herself, but Wes calls Rose as soon as he is alone. "Listen, Rose," he says. "Laurie has resigned because of a personal problem with one of the men in the unit. Find out as much as you can about it because I'd like to discuss this situation with you this afternoon."

Rose and Laurie go looking for one another, and they have lunch together that day. During the meal, Laurie tells Rose why she resigned. She does not use Carl's name, but she does say yes when Rose asks her if Carl is the man in her story. And Rose learns from Laurie that she was embarrassed to tell Wes exactly what Carl had said. Laurie does tell Rose all the details.

∽०∾

INSTRUCTIONS AND QUESTIONS

You are Rose Wong, and you are on your way to Wes Jennings's office. You guess that Wes wants to talk about Carl, and this is not the first time. When Wanda Blake started working in your unit, she complained about Carl following her home after work, phoning her at home, and following her when she was on dates with other men.

You are aware of Carl's opinion of his sexual prowess, but you have never heard of his threatening anyone. Knowing of the incident with Laurie, what do you do now? Why?

42

Conflicts on the Human Services Coordination Team

The meeting he dreads will begin in less than an hour, so Jerry Feldman reluctantly takes out the files on Arthur Harris and Frances Carpenter for one last review.

As Director of Field Services for the Human Services Coordination Team of the State Services Department (SSD), Jerry supervises both people. Arthur is Northeast Regional Director, and Frances is Arthur's specialist in inner-city problems. The team's mission is to work with citizens' groups, private agencies, other public agencies, and SSD's own program divisions, to coordinate the targeting of social services and to increase citizen involvement in their delivery. A major part of that mission involves identifying individuals and groups that need specific services and assisting them in making claims on those best able to meet their needs. The team's activities are conducted in five regions, and the field staffs in each region average a half-dozen professionals and two clericals. Headquarters for the team is the SSD office in the capital, but Jerry spends a lot of time on the road visiting the regional offices, which are the central units of the team.

The regional directors, like Arthur Harris, have multiple responsibilities. They develop work assignments for their subordinates and maintain communication among them so they do not work at cross-purposes. Also, they develop the strategies and priorities for headquarters, implement them in the field, evaluate staff, and make recommendations for promotions, terminations, or reassignments. Furthermore, they supervise the administrative details that arise from the constant travel of the field workers. The nature of the team's mission is such that the regional directors have to supervise their subordinates closely and give them more corrective feedback than is common in most social-service work. After all, the team's mission is coordination, and that means that its own staff should be the best coordinated of all.

Arthur Harris's file reveals that he has been a member of the team since it was authorized a year and a half earlier, all that time in the northeast region. The details reveal that Arthur is a real up and comer. After three years in the Army, he had completed his bachelor's degree with a double major in sociology and political science. He did one year of graduate work in sociology before taking a planning position elsewhere in the department. Selected for the team because of interest and performance, Arthur receives generally good evaluations and reflects increasing interest in "street-level" administration. Arthur is among the younger employees expected to rise to positions of considerable responsibility in the department. He is white.

Frances Carpenter is quite different from Arthur. She is seven years older, has two children, has completed about two years' college credit, and is black. Her interest in street-level administration is not new. Before joining the Human Services Coordination Team at the same time Arthur did, she was a community-relations specialist with the Community Action Program in Benton, which with its sister city of Fillmore constitutes the major urban center of the northeast region. Almost everyone in Benton knows Frances's name, and in the black community of about 15,000 there are few people who do not know her personally. She led a well-publicized rent strike, worked for community control of the police, and helped initiate compensatory programs for the disadvantaged in Benton County Community College. Her specialty in the northeast region is working with the black communities of Benton and Fillmore.

Jerry found her to be capable at the start. She is the best person in the region for handling service delivery foul-ups, both because she knows the right people and because she is inventive at creating constructive responses. Evaluations of her performance during the first year are positive. Arthur Harris's predecessor as regional director was an older black man who left the job for a top position in post-release correctional services. He knew Frances for many years, and they worked well together.

Jerry feared that some trouble might develop when he promoted Arthur Harris, even though Arthur seemed to have support from each of his co-workers. Initially, Arthur worked out well, but, after a couple of months, friction developed between Frances and Arthur, who began to write that Frances was resisting direction. He even entered notes in her file that she failed to carry out an assignment that he requested her to undertake. Other notes—none part of the permanent record—indicate that Frances frequently gets into arguments with other staff members, all of whom are white. And most recently, she missed two weekly meetings of the field staff without notice or explanation.

When Arthur told her that if she missed a third consecutive staff meeting he would consider giving her a written reprimand, Frances blew up, called him a racist and sexist incompetent in tones that could be heard by anyone nearby, stormed out of the office, and disappeared for a day and a half. She returned to the office in a subdued manner with a signed agreement by a voluntary agency to open a day-care center in the inner city of Benton. That was a good piece of work.

But Arthur still feels he needs Jerry's intervention, and hence the scheduled meeting to which Jerry is not looking forward.

Frances arrives first in the regional office's conference room. Jerry asks her to have a seat. "Good to see you," he says. "I heard about your blowup with Arthur the other day and thought the three of us ought to get together. You've worked together for long enough that an incident like this is cause for concern. Do you want to talk for a few minutes before Arthur comes in, or would you rather wait?"

"Oh, I don't know," she replies. "I'm sorry I yelled and got him upset, but he's really been after me. I used to think he was understanding, but now I'm not sure. He tries hard, but he's not as grown up as he thinks, and he's been putting on a lot of airs."

"What do you mean?" Jerry asks.

"You know, playing like he's the big boss with all these evaluations. I've worked here as long as he has, and I know my job. He should be helpful, but instead he's always trying to act superior."

"What kind of things does he do to act superior?" Jerry inquires.

"Well, you know, Mr. Feldman, like always trying to pretend he knows better than I do what's happening in Benton, like he knows the needs there. He gives me a lot of things from books and then tries to make me feel like it's my fault, not his, when they don't work."

"Like what?"

"Like the time he wanted me to get young mothers organized for prenatal care," Frances explains. "You can't change kids' habits like that. Some are 14-year-olds hardly aware of what's happening to them. I tried a little, but there are so many other things to do, it wasn't worth the effort right then. A time will come for that. If Arthur really knew the black community here in Benton, he'd understand that."

They are interrupted by a knock on the door. "Is that you, Arthur? Come on in," Jerry calls.

Arthur is a little nervous and awkward as he sits down. He smiles at Frances and then asks Jerry how things are at headquarters. After a brief reply, Jerry suggests that they get down to business. "Why don't each of you tell what you think is going on? Arthur, do you want to go first?"

"Well, if that's the way you would like to proceed," Arthur offers. "I think this is a very complicated situation with a lot of elements in it."

Arthur pauses and thinks for a minute. "I respect Frances a lot, and I'm a little uneasy saying some of this because we have worked together as equals before I became her supervisor."

"I have an idea," Jerry interrupts. "Why don't you talk to Frances as well as to me? After all, whatever is going on, and whatever we manage to do here today, you two are still going to have to work things out between you."

"All right," Arthur responds. "Before I became your supervisor, when the office first opened, Frances, we worked mostly on helping people caught between the cracks in social services or people getting a bureaucratic pass-me-around—you know, case kinds of things. I don't know if you have an equal around here in handling that kind of matter."

"Well," Frances says with feigned surprise, "that's the first time you have ever admitted that!"

"Hmmm," Jerry murmurs. "Continue?"

"All right," Arthur says. "You know, casework isn't all that we should be doing. Our real goal is human-services integration. I've felt that one of the reasons I was promoted, Jerry, was because you felt that I could help this region get more into programmatic activities, you know, the kinds of things where, instead of helping a few people, we implement a change that will help lots of people now and into the future.

"It's been my goal to try to do that," Arthur continues. "Things like helping service-delivery agencies establish good coordinative mechanisms between city agencies or between the county and the department, for example. We shouldn't do all the coordination, we should be setting it up so other people do that. Isn't that right, Jerry?"

"That's one of the objectives. Yes, certainly," Jerry replies.

"Well, I've tried to do that since becoming regional director," Arthur says as he looks back at Frances. "For some reason—I don't know why—you've always seemed to resist that idea."

"That's not true," Frances says.

"You'll get your turn," Jerry cautions. "Go on, Arthur, and remember to tell Frances your thoughts."

"My feeling is that both your experience and your talents lead you to prefer casework," Arthur continues.

Frances looks upset.

"Wait a minute," Jerry says. "Let's try and avoid motivations and interpretations. Just describe what happened. We'll look for causes in due time."

Arthur agrees and goes on. "The first few suggestions I gave you just seemed to bounce right off and disappear, Frances. I suggested that you try to improve coordination between County Probation and the summer softball programs in Benton County. You said you didn't know anyone in the athletic programs and that they didn't work in the city. Then there was the business with developing support in the Fillmore City Council for community-based mental-health halfway houses, which nothing ever came of. I tried to talk to you about that and tried to get you to set down on paper your goals for the next six months. But you never did. Instead, you gave me a lot of excuses about how busy you were. Then you began getting into arguments a lot during the last two or three months and...."

"What do you mean, a lot?" Frances retorts. "And besides, I didn't have many arguments, just a few disagreements."

"Man, if those weren't arguments, I don't know!" Arthur notes with an exaggerated shrug.

Jerry laughs. "What's an argument to you, Arthur?"

"That's kind of hard to define," he says. "I guess when people start getting heated over their disagreements."

"What about you?" Jerry asks Frances.

"Well, both people at least have to start yelling. If my ears don't hurt it's not much of an argument," she responds.

"OK," Jerry says. "What happened next?"

"I don't know," Arthur says. "Things just started to go downhill. I feel that Frances just hasn't kept up with the others in terms of program improvements. I tried to get her to see this at the weekly staff meetings by having other people talk about what they were doing."

"That was an attempt to put me down," Frances asserts.

"Hold on," Jerry says. "Let's keep motives out of it. How did you feel? That's the question."

"Well," she says, "I felt angry. He never wanted to...."

"Tell it to Arthur," Jerry reminds her.

"Man, you are something," Frances says. "All right, *you* never wanted to hear about what I was doing. I was doing a lot of things. I got the locations changed on the health clinics, and I found a way to get hot meals for the old folks, and I steered a group of kids into a teen center they never knew existed, and a whole lot of other things. But all those meetings were a lot of talk about bureaucratic I-don't-know-what. I thought I was supposed to work against that, not make more of it!"

"That's just the point," Arthur says. "If we don't make these agencies work right, then no one will get the services they need. I know you mean well, but in the long run this way is better for the black community and all the people."

"What do you know about the black community?" Frances shoots back. "Have you ever lived there? That's what I'm supposed to know. If you knew anything about the black community you'd know better what is an argument and what isn't."

"Well, when someone stomps around an office picking fights and contradicting everyone, that's an argument," Arthur says.

"Oh, you and your bourgeois standards," Frances replies. "What do you know? I have a right to get upset once in a while," she says assertively. "Besides, what am I supposed to do? There's no one in that office I can talk to. Everyone's so concerned with doing good they never bother to find out what the people are like."

"You don't have any monopoly on the people," Arthur responds. "We work with lots of different kinds of people. It's not just the black community, and you have to understand that."

"I think we are getting diverted from the main issue," Jerry proposes. "Why don't you tell Arthur more about his idea of programs?"

"Well, he's got some problems about black folks that need some work, but all right." She turns back to Arthur. "I never did understand all that program stuff. I remember about the softball leagues, but I don't know any of those people. When I came to you about that, you just gave me some names to call. Well I had already got the names! And I tried to talk to people in Fillmore, and they gave me the run-around. They're a lot of racists over there, and you never should have asked me to deal with them. Charlie Welsh knows all those people. Why don't you ask him?"

"That's just the point. You have to expand your base of operations if you are going to become programmatic," Arthur says. "You should be able to deal with all kinds of situations. If you are going to get good evaluation reports, you have to do the same as all the other field officers."

"Who's doing the evaluations? You?" Frances asks. "How are you going to evaluate me? You don't understand the black community, and you don't know our needs. I was hired to work on the things I know best," Frances states. "And that's what I do. You got all these fancy ideas about programs and all that bureaucratic stuff, but you don't understand blacks or how to evaluate us. You don't understand me enough to help me when I ask for it, so how can you evaluate me? All you do is put me down at staff meetings, then you wonder why I don't come and threaten you with reprimands and all that."

"I certainly can evaluate you and your work," Arthur maintains. "I use the same standards that I use to evaluate anyone's work. There's no difference between black or white. This isn't a race issue, and I resent your trying to make it one," Arthur snaps.

"Well, that's where you're wrong," Frances responds. "If you think you just go out and hang the same standards on all people, you *are* a racist and you don't even know it!" Frances yells. "You call yourself a supervisor and think you can evaluate me? You don't even know what I do, and you don't even care. All you care about is your so-called program plans, and I don't need any of that white middle-class stuff that's been keeping black people down for years!"

☙◦❧

INSTRUCTIONS AND QUESTIONS

You are Jerry. A welcome emergency long-distance call gets you off the spot for a few moments. You steal a few more minutes to reflect on the meeting. So far, the discussion has ventilated some issues, and things are beginning to get hot.

1. As Jerry, where would you like to see the discussion go from here?

2. How do you think you have handled the conflict so far, and what would you have done differently?

3. What do you think you have done well about directing the discussion?

4. You tick off some of the issues. Is Arthur racist? Do you think he understands the "black community?" Do you think there *is* such a thing? Should Frances be evaluated or otherwise treated differently from the other members of the field staff?

5. You also are aware of the differences of opinion and values between Arthur and Frances. Which are proper subjects for management concern? Should you try to help find a way toward a resolution of their conflict that helps each better understand the other's goals and needs and still is consistent with the agency's mission and the community's needs?

6. With these thoughts in mind, what is your opening intervention to be when you reenter the conference room? How do you expect Frances will respond? Arthur?

43

The Making of a Corrections Officer

Chuck Bronson is the head of the law-enforcement division in Harrison. It is with considerable satisfaction that he keeps hearing glowing reports from his chief of police about the efficiency and smooth operation of the division.

This pat on the back is gratifying to Chuck for more than one reason. Several months ago, when he took over the division, things were being handled on a day-to-day and crisis-to-crisis basis. Major intraoffice jealousies had existed for some time. Much of the office resources were being wasted and misused. Chuck also came into the job with two strikes against him. He was given a pay grade and rank one step lower than the position called for, and he was younger than many of his staff employees. His enthusiasm for enforcement work and his thorough background and training in enforcement procedures, along with a lot of long hours and hard work, finally paid off. Chuck has made a personal goal of running things smoothly enough so crises can be handled without sacrificing long-range planning. He believes he has succeeded. Now intraoffice relationships are cordial and productive, and his staff often "reads" him well enough to understand what he wants before he asks for it. He considers his chances for promotion to be excellent, particularly if he stays in his present position long enough to reap the benefits of some hard work.

SITUATION 1

The outer-office phone rings, and Chuck's secretary notifies him on the intercom that the chief wants to see him right away. Walking to the chief's office, Chuck wonders what big crisis has come up now.

The big crisis involves Chuck, as he guesses from the unusually somber expression on the chief's face. The chief is abrupt. "How do you feel about taking over the corrections division next week?" Although caught off guard, Chuck begins to detail the reasons he cannot possibly accept. He has no expertise in corrections, his expertise in enforcement would be wasted, the present corrections officer has prior experience, and some of Chuck's pending projects for the enforcement division might not reach fruition if he is suddenly moved.

The chief interrupts by saying: "I know all of that, Chuck. I know especially that you've got a lot of time and effort invested where you are and that you prefer to say there." But the chief's need is compelling:

"I have got to get the corrections division straightened out. The man in the job, regardless of his past experience, isn't producing results.

"You will have experienced staff people to work with. I'm counting on your organizational ability and the fact that you are a strict disciplinarian to assist you in ironing things out. I'm sorry I can't give you much of an idea what's wrong with the corrections shop. Since you'll have to spend this next week finishing up current work in your office, you won't have time for any prior look into it either. I do know the prisoners are practically running the jail, that the guards won't take positive action, and that the mayor is afraid of a riot almost anytime now.

"I'll be out of town at a convention next week when you go over there, but I'll notify the division that you are coming to take charge next week. The present corrections officer will stay there a couple of days to show you the operation and introduce you to the key staff members."

Chuck is fighting a losing battle, and he knows it.

"Yes sir," he answers. He realizes that the decision was made before he entered the office and that nothing he can say now is going to change anything, except to rile the Old Man. Besides, he is flattered by the chief's confidence in him.

∽○∾

INSTRUCTIONS AND QUESTIONS

1. What mistakes has the chief made in motivating Chuck toward his new job?

2. Admitting that Chuck may have been the best choice to replace the old corrections officer, how could the chief have better assisted Chuck in assuming his new position?

3. Given only the information above, what do you think Chuck's initial approach to the new job should be?

SITUATION 2

During his first day in the corrections division, Chuck sits in on a meeting called by the outgoing corrections officer and attended by all section chiefs and other key staff personnel. The corrections officer briefly introduces him as "my replacement." Chuck says only that he is looking forward to working with everyone in his new position.

As the meeting progresses and he becomes less the focus of attention and open curiosity, Chuck looks around the room and notes that many of the staff are older. He already knows that many of them have extensive experience in the corrections field and that a good percentage have worked in their present jobs for some time.

The meeting is suddenly interrupted when the corrections officer is advised that a prisoner in the main cellblock refuses to go on work detail until he has spoken with the corrections officer personally. The corrections officer immediately adjourns the meeting, saying that it will be continued later, and leaves for the cellblock. As the staff members leave the room, Chuck overhears the following comments:

"Happens every time we try to have a meeting and get something done."

"Yeah, whatever the prisoners want they get and right when they want it, too."

"I wonder if this new guy will be like the old one and try to bribe the prisoners into being good."

"I hope not."

"Procedures are laid down by the department to help us control the prisoners, and then the top man violates them the worst."

For the remainder of the first day and all of the second day, Chuck tours the administrative office and jail complex and reads written procedures dealing with division operations, including the rule books for guards and prisoners. The procedures outlined seem workable, yet Chuck notices that many of them are not being followed. The guards in the main cellblock, for example, exercise little control over the prisoners; cells are not maintained properly by the prisoners; and guards and administrative personnel alike seem disinterested in doing anything about it. On one occasion, a prisoner requests and receives from the corrections officer permission to do something that he has just been told by a guard he couldn't do. The prisoner thanks the corrections officer, smiles at the guard, and strolls off down the corridor. The guard looks questioningly at the corrections officer and then, with an expression of defeat, walks away. Chuck also notices that the departing corrections officer is everywhere—almost constantly involved in the work his subordinates should be doing.

On his first day as the corrections officer, Chuck calls a meeting of the key staff personnel. Sensing wariness and uncertainty on the part of the group, he decides to attack the problem directly. He begins a brief talk:

> Although I've been here only a short time, I have observed certain things, which I feel need correcting. I'll admit, as many of you may already know, that I have no experience in corrections work. I have, however, thoroughly read the procedures outlined for this division's operation and feel that the sooner we begin following them the better.
>
> In fact, I want all of the section chiefs to review the written procedures. I expect to see them fully implemented by the end of the week.
>
> I have already observed too many people who seem to have little or no interest in their work. Guards have little control over the prisoners, and office personnel spend more time drinking coffee than processing paperwork. I have personally witnessed occasions when the former corrections officer was unable to do his own work because of the time spent in the various sections doing some of your jobs for you.
>
> I overhead a comment the other day expressing concern about whether I would be soft with the prisoners. Don't worry about that while I'm here. I can be a pretty strict disciplinarian, when necessary.
>
> Let me also make it clear, however, that firm standards will apply to the staff as well as to the prisoners.
>
> Most of you probably know that I was sent here because of the chief's and the mayor's concern about the lack of efficiency; in fact, I was told to straighten this operation out. That is what I intend to do. I will make daily tours throughout the facility to become more acquainted with each of you and your jobs and to see how you are implementing the guidance I've outlined today.
>
> I think that is enough for our first meeting. Are there any questions?

At Chuck's question, a couple of the senior section chiefs exchange glances, the rest of the group sit looking at him without expression, and no one speaks. "Well, I guess your silence means that you have no questions, so let's all get back to work. There's a lot of it to be done."

As the staff silently files out of his office, Chuck hopes that his little talk really builds a fire under some of these people and gets the division on its way to running smoothly.

INSTRUCTIONS AND QUESTIONS

1. What mistakes, if any, has Chuck made in the first formal contact with his new staff?
2. Has he repeated any of the same mistakes made by the chief last week in dealing with him?
3. To what do you attribute the fact that the group raised no questions after Chuck's comments?
4. Does it appear that Chuck is correct in assuming that the problems of the corrections division are being caused by personnel with little interest in doing their jobs correctly?

SITUATION 3

Over the next few days, Chuck makes a point of visiting the facility's various sections. In each of them he is treated with courtesy, but he feels none of the real "contact" with the personnel that he experienced with his former staff. Section chiefs and first-line supervisors become particularly edgy when he mentions the subject of following the written procedures, and when he asks if they are having any problems or when he asks whether things are going better now that the guidelines are being followed, he uniformly receives the same response—an unenthusiastic, "Yes, sir, everything's going just fine."

Chuck notes that, while the procedures are being followed, there does not seem to be much improvement in overall attitude. Guards and office personnel continue to exhibit a casual, almost disinterested, concern for their work. The shoulder-to-the-wheel attitude, which he hoped for as a result of his first meeting, is still lacking.

Unable to put his finger on what the problem is, Chuck returns to his office and decides to seek other opinions. He calls in Sergeant Brown, his chief assistant, for a private talk. Brown has a wealth of experience, and Chuck has already noticed that the sergeant is held in high esteem by co-workers. Chuck also appreciates that Brown has made a special effort to relieve him of some of the routine office matters until he gets his feet more firmly on the ground. Chuck feels that Brown might be willing to assist him. Chuck says:

> Sergeant Brown, the fact that there seems to be no improvement in attitude among the staff as a result of my meeting the other day concerns me a great deal.

You and I both know that people who are happy with their work do a better job, and this is what really solves problems. The written procedures are being followed as I directed, but conditions are not much better.

I'm beginning to feel that I've gotten off on the wrong foot with the staff and that my original assessment of the overall problem may have been an error.

I want you to level with me and tell me what you think the problems are. Also, since I realize, because of my inexperience, that I need the willing help of the staff, please give me your ideas on how I can better work with them to gain their cooperation and support.

∽०∼

INSTRUCTIONS AND QUESTIONS

1. Does it appear that Chuck's approach with Brown is better or worse than the one he used with the whole group in the earlier meeting? Why?

2. Is Chuck showing a weakness as a manager in his discussion with Brown?

3. Do you think that a similar approach would have been wise for the first meeting with the whole group?

44

Distributing County Property Without Consent

Dan Nicholas decides to promote Susan Maier to head the business office of a local community work release program. In her new position, Susan has two employees to supervise directly, Jan Miller, an employee of two years, and Paula Nicholas, a new employee just completing half of her probationary period and awaiting an interim performance appraisal before being granted permanent status. Dan informs Susan that one of her first supervisory tasks is to conduct Paula's performance evaluation.

Less than two weeks later, Susan and Paula sit down to discuss Paula's evaluation. During the evaluation, it becomes very evident that Susan is unhappy with Paula's performance. Paula receives below-average scores and is described by Susan as being "insolent." The episode ends with Paula feeling very uncomfortable about the future of her position, and she is upset by the terminology used to describe her behavior. She is also very disturbed by the low scores. The next day, Paula confides in her co-worker about the evaluation. Jan shares Paula's belief that she was being wrongly treated. Later that day, Susan becomes aware of Jan's and Paula's ill feelings through the office grapevine but does nothing to resolve the dispute.

The next day, while reading through the instructions for the new computer system the office had just obtained, Paula found two sets of stickers that attach to the keys of the new computer keyboard. The stickers, when attached to the keyboard, indicate what that individual key's function is. Paula, thinking that these stickers would be of great use on her own personal computer at home, keeps one set for herself and gives the other set to Jan. The next day when Paula arrives at work, she finds herself facing disciplinary action for "distributing county property without her supervisor's consent."

INSTRUCTIONS AND QUESTIONS

You are Dan Nicholas. You realize that you fought long and hard to get the extra position in the business office to ease the workload burden. Paula was the person hired to fill that position. It will take at least six months to fill the position again if Paula resigns or is forced out. On the other hand, you promoted Susan to the supervisory position over the objections of your boss.

What do you do now? You have scheduled a 10:00 A.M. meeting with Susan and it is now less than one hour away.

45

Easing Toward Change in Urbania's Finance Department

Urbania is a city of about 250,000 people located in the Northeast. Four major industrial corporations bring it international attention, and it has several widely admired programs among its institutions of higher education. For many years it has had a manager-council form of government, and several of its recent managers have gone on to prominent positions elsewhere. A new, highly respected city manager took office in the early '90s. After much coaxing, he finally convinced Lee Edwards to join his staff as finance director.

In his previous job, Edwards had found primitive conditions. He rushed the city into modern finance by making major personnel changes, even though his hands were often tied in the choice of systems and policies. In that job, for example, state law mandated an accounting system—widely acknowledged as a major impediment to modern management. The finance director was still depositing money in no-interest bank accounts. Edwards did what he could. He simply forced out the key division heads and replaced them with his own "elite cadre" of modern finance officers. The elite worked a bit harder to make up for weaknesses throughout the system, and this strategy worked well enough.

In Urbania, unlike in his previous job, Edwards has a base to work from. He decides that he will fight rather than switch. The fiscal operations are hardly modern, and Edwards finds a finance department filled with advanced bureaucrats. However, one division chief has to be moved out, and the rest seem trainable.

Edwards has several concerns about his finance department. One is technical, the other social. Urbania still backs up all computer transactions on paper, a very time-consuming and labor-intensive process. For example, each transaction and each document must be carefully checked at each step in processing, especially whenever any posting is done. Because paperwork is built around manual files, there are redundant forms as well as redundant checkpoints. The latter are still necessary in today's electronic era, but the former are not. It is better to assign numbers to each transaction and control that file number than to control the paperwork associated with it. That means greater control at entry and less control along the processing path.

What does Edwards want, basically? He seeks, among other reforms, a reduction and consolidation of forms. He also wants greater efficiency from his staff. Finally, he wants a staff that can take responsibility for the quality and efficiency of its own work. Few of the staff have ever worked anywhere except the city government. He characterizes them as "beaten down" and "bureaucratized."

In order to make the changes he wants, Edwards needs the active support of his staff. That requires, as he sees it, their understanding of what their work is and how well they do it. So, for several months he patiently assembles data about the finance department. Finally, he has a transaction log—a summary of all the transactions that the department has processed during the past year. Except for executive functions like planning bond issues, the staff still process too much paper. The electronic transaction log summarizes what kinds of things have been done, in what volumes, and with what degree of efficiency.

Edwards has a report prepared and calls a meeting of all his division and section heads. His goals? The department processes 13 forms, each with a different number that is coded into the transaction number and fed into the accounting system. Edwards knows that this number of forms must be reduced. He wants the staff to suggest how.

At the meeting, Edwards asks for comments on the data that had never before been available. In the past 12 months the department has processed 135,624 transactions. Of those, 10,757 were rejected on the first pass, and 124,867 were accepted, for an overall error rate of about 8 percent. In setting up the initial budget accounts or making transfers among them, 1,192 documents involving 8,346 first-pass transactions result in 484 rejections—over 5 percent. About 10 percent of the purchase orders are rejected on the first pass, and contracts—for which there is a separate encumbrance procedure—have a 20 percent error rate. Edwards notes to the assembled staff that for 250 workdays per annum, they make an average of 40 errors a day.

For several hours, the staff discusses the data and the error rates. As the day passes, Edwards steers the conversation around to the forms. He asks how the department could reduce the number of forms to a minimum?

The staff defends the existing forms for some time, as Edwards had expected. After all, he reasons, they do a pretty good job for the most part. The error rates are lower than in many cities. The vendors are paid, the taxes assessed, and the ledgers of receivables are kept up-to-date. Things could be worse, and the staff knows it. Edwards seeks to bring them to a new level of consciousness about their systems, not simply to bring them up to some minimum standard.

After another hour or so, the group climate opens a little. Edwards feels that he can begin presenting specific issues for group resolution. He begins with one specific form, the journal voucher form. He wants to consolidate it with others into a multipurpose form.

Briefly, he outlines his wish, then throws the matter open for discussion. First he turns to Frank Paterno, the director of the accounting division.

"What do you think, Frank?" Edwards asks earnestly. "Perhaps you have some arguments against consolidating the form; you will be the one who has the most responsibility in using the form if it's changed."

"You just let me know what you want, Mr. Edwards, and I'll make it work," Paterno responds.

"That's not the point, Frank," Edwards says. "I want to know what you think."

"Aw, Mr. Edwards, you make the policy here. I just make it work as best I can. I'm with you 100 percent in anything you want to do. You know, I want this to be the best finance department in the state. That's why all you have to do is let me know what you need. The manager would not have you here if you weren't the best."

"Thank you Frank; that's very kind," Edwards responds. "Let me try something a little more specific. I really would like your opinions on this matter. Do you think that consolidating the form will speed up processing? Or reduce the error rate?"

"Naw, it won't be any trouble, Mr. Edwards. It might take a few days to get used to, but we're going to get the error rate way down. And I promise you that, either way, my staff will move those vouchers faster. So you just let me know your preference, and I'll make it work," Paterno persists.

"Can you think of any troubles a new consolidated form might cause, Frank?" Edwards shows that he can also be persistent.

"Not if it's your wish, Chief," replies Paterno. "There can't be any problems my staff can't handle. I'm really proud of them and know they want you to have the best damn accounting division there is."

"Do you think your section heads will share your enthusiasm for whatever I want?" Edwards asks.

Paterno looks around at his section heads and smiles. They smile back nervously. "Of course they will, Mr. Edwards. I think I can speak for them on this matter. We really appreciate meeting like this and learning your ideas. Nobody in the past has taken the time to explain their plans to us. You can trust us to live up to your confidence in us. You can bet on that."

"Thank you, Frank. But I'd like to ask them directly for their views. Of course, your support is important to me in this," Edwards concludes.

He turns to Joan Prosper, one of Paterno's more outspoken section heads. "What do you think?" Edwards asks her.

"Frank's right," she replies. "You let us know, and we'll make it work. If we have trouble, I hope you'll help us. But that shouldn't be necessary. It doesn't sound like anything we can't handle."

A few of Paterno's staffers join in, tentatively at first. Florence Richardson offers that she does not know much about this kind of issue. Jo Simmons thinks it is really nice to be part of important changes.

Edwards smiles positively, thanks each of them, and breaks the pencil he holds between his fingers under the table.

Finally he turns to Gwen Rivera, the last of Paterno's section heads. "Well, that brings us to Gwen. What do you think?" Edwards asks.

"If we change the form," she notes, "we'll have no easy place where we can keep both the debits and the credits. They'll get lost on a big form. The way it is now, you have one place where you can always check both sides of the transaction, and this new way we won't have it so clear. That's what I think," Rivera blurts out and stops. She looks around at the others nervously.

Someone from budget control meekly agrees with Rivera.

Simmons, upon prodding, admits that Rivera has a point, and Richardson feels that if Simmons and Rivera both think that way then maybe the group should discuss it further. Prosper chips in with additional supporting reasons why the form might be retained, at the same time offering a few reasons why it should be consolidated. Paterno sits uncomfortably.

"Thank you, ladies," Edwards continues. "Those are some good points. I had not thought about them before. Frank, what do you think now?"

"Just the same as before, Chief. I think we can make it work. You just let us know what we can do to help out and count on us to contribute. These are small points that won't be any obstacle if you want to use the new form. My staff can do it for you, just you watch," Paterno concludes.

"I'll tell you what," Edwards tries. "Let's put it to a vote, right here in this room. You have heard the pros and cons. A vote will indicate the overall sentiment. Frank, why don't you start the voting?"

Paterno responds pertly. "I'll vote with you, he says.

"But I haven't voted yet," Edwards says.

That is OK with Paterno, apparently. "Whichever way you vote, I'll vote that way too."

"No dice, Frank. You have to vote yes or no," replies Edwards.

"Come on, Frank" says Prosper. "You have to let us know how you vote."

"Whichever way Mr. Edwards wants, that's how," Paterno snaps.

"You have to take a position, Frank," says Edwards. "Now how is it, yes or no?"

༄

INSTRUCTIONS AND QUESTIONS

1. What is going on in Paterno's mind? Why is he reluctant to vote?
2. As Edwards, what can you do to get Paterno to express an opinion, to "open him up"?
3. Comment on Edwards's strategy of feeding back aggregate data about the finance function as a means of fostering organizational change. What are the likely benefits and risks? What else might Edwards do to accomplish his goals of transforming the technical and the social system of the finance department?
4. Why do you think Paterno is so reluctant to open up to Edwards? Do you think it is wise for Paterno to act this way?
5. What are Edwards's assumptions about the people working for him? What theory or model of leadership is he working from? How does he expect his new workers to react?
6. How do you think a vote on the new forms would turn out? Why?
7. Would you use Edwards's approach with this group? Why (not)?
8. What theories support your approach?

46

"Keep a Two-by-Four Behind Your Desk"

You are the assistant city manager of Academic City, and this year you are in charge of budget preparations. Why you? The finance director is retiring and her replacement has not yet been recruited. Moreover, the budget director is new to the job. In this manager-council city of 100,000 citizens, the budget has traditionally been the domain of the manager and finance director. The budget director's position was added several years ago when the clerical, administrative, and accounting details of budget making began to distract the manager and finance director from the important budget decisions. The organization of the city government is still rather loose and informal.

It's February, and you have sent out the budget instructions to the departments. You call in Lester Standeford, the budget director, to tell him how you and the manager will make the budget this year. This year, you tell Standeford, you are going to continue opening up the budget process, just as you have been doing for several years. You want the process to produce as much information as possible about costs, service requirements, citizen demands, trade-offs, and downstream consequences. The city manager intends to make recommendations to the council that are supported as fully as possible with appropriate and accurate data. You want the council to have the same kind of information, so it can change the manager's recommendations and feel confident in doing so.

You have this conversation because you do not trust Standeford to do exactly what you assign him to do. Last year was Standeford's first budget cycle, and he seemed resistant to the city manager's desire to open up the budget process. The finance director was willing to make some moves in that direction, but not as far or as fast as the manager desired. Given the finance director's impending retirement, the manager had not pushed her hard on this matter. In any case, Standeford had been sheltered from the full understanding of the ways budgets would be made from then on.

So this year you are telling Standeford straight out what his job will be. You and the city manager want Standeford to produce "De-Em-Eye"—decision-making information. You and the manager are making recommendations based on that information. The council is the representative body; you and the manager are going to make sure it can act responsibly. You know that you have an unusually good council right now and believe that for the next few years this city can work like a textbook-case council-manager city.

Standeford seems to have trouble getting the message. He likes to produce conclusions and hold onto information.

Now it's March. The estimates have been coming in from the departments. You call Standeford in and tell him that he is to check out all the estimates for conformity with forms and instructions. You want him to verify numerical accuracy and identify any unusual increases, decreases, or other anomalies.

The next Monday morning Standeford is in your office with a folder full of papers. He says he has done the work you requested and has a number of recommendations. He tells you that the city really ought to switch from Chevrolets to Dodges for its fleet: Dodges have become a really good car, and the prices are "rock bottom." The city ought to buy a couple of the new Macintosh computers; they are really hot stuff and have great software. Several of his friends have them at home and love them. Standeford goes on. You try to stop this torrent of words but can't without being sarcastic or authoritarian.

Standeford continues:

Oh, yes, I have some other recommendations. You know, about those bullet-proof vests the cops want? Well, I think if they want them they ought to buy them just like they do their own uniforms. We don't have a uniform allowance here, and we pay the cops pretty well. The crime rate here isn't so high that vests are a necessity, they are really a luxury. And we have no room in this budget for luxury. No sir!

And the same is true for the library. I mean, you know, when was the last time you used the library, anyway? I haven't been in it since I moved here and none of my friends ever go there either. The schools all have libraries for the kids and the college has a library. I mean, why should we increase book acquisition spending by 18 percent?

And the other big one here is, you know, that land-banking program that Parks and Rec wants. You know, let's be serious. This city needs a tax base and nobody is having kids like they used to. We already have more park space than Stevens Falls or Birmingham or Primavera. I guess we can't cut it out completely in one year, but I blue-penciled the bog property and the Webster Junction parcel and Copper Avenue. You know Copper Avenue—we ought to make sure Bryce Development gets that before the residents get wind of the possibility of a park there and we lose the ratables that parcel could bring! Bryce will put forty units on a parcel that size. You know what that means in property taxes?

"Thanks a lot, Lester," you say wearily. "But I don't think you have given me what I asked for. The kinds of recommendations you're making are things we need to bring up to council. We're not going to decide them on the basis of your likes and dislikes.

"If you can produce some hard information, decision-making information—I'm happy to have it. Like just what is the trend in library utilization? And why do the police want the vests? How many shootings have we had and what is the trend and how much would it really cost to save one life? As for the land bank, just keep out of that one altogether, do you understand? The council authorized it and has supported it every year. I've kept them fully informed on the fiscal impacts and they love the program.

"My job is to inform the council, not to slip things by them. Do you get my point?" you explain to Lester.

"And, by the way, when you bring me back your report and the rest of the stuff, do an analysis of the cash capital request from Parks and Recreation, will you? I need to know *why* some parks are programmed for more small projects than others. I want data, not recommendations. What does it cost to mow each park, which park has more buildings to maintain, what types of use do we have in the major ones, what are the utilization patterns and volumes, you know? Information, got it? Now will you go do some work that *I* need done and stop trying to do my job? Get it?"

You sink back into your chair and sigh. What am I going to do with this guy? You remember what the manager had said last year. "With guys like Lester," he said, "sometimes you just have to keep a big two-by-four behind your desk and every once in a while just beat them over the head!"

Two days after his unsatisfying meeting with you, Lester Standeford is back. He enters your office with a file folder in one hand and, it seems, is already talking.

About those capital projects in Parks you wanted me to look at. Well, in Hamlin Park—out where I live—they want to put in four drinking fountains in the northwest section to serve the softball backstops they put in last year. Now that's the old park where they have those lovely old fountains. You know the ones, with the flagstone enclosures and real porcelain bowls and those really ornate faucets?

Well, I mean, I called a friend who works in plumbing and he tells me we can still get those faucets and bowls—they come as a set, you know? They just are not that expensive compared to the ugly standpipes that Kelly in Parks has proposed. I mean, I know it takes a little money for the flagstone enclosures, but it's really worth the difference to maintain the architectural integrity of a place like Hamlin Park. I've already called Kelly to let him know that I'm recommending this change to you...."

∽o∾

INSTRUCTIONS AND QUESTIONS

You reach behind you for that mythical two-by-four with which to swat Standeford. Is he dumb, insubordinate, or crazy?

1. What are you going to do with him right now, and later on? How are you going to get him to do the staff work you need to make the budget process work properly?
2. While you are at it, outline your plan for how you are trying to run the budget this year. Maybe Standeford isn't the only one having trouble following what you and city manager are attempting to do.
3. You want to make sure that you don't get too far ahead of the players. Perhaps you need to give some attention to possible differences between the theory you espouse and the theory you and others practice. What are the differences you can identify?

47

"Stop Having Birthdays!"

ROGER: And the next time you plan a birthday luncheon for me, make damn sure you tell me about it first. It's off. I'm not going today or any other day.

CATHERINE: Well, if you don't want any more luncheons, stop having birthdays!

ROGER: And I've had enough of your one-line comebacks. You may think it's funny, but I'm not joking. Just don't consider me a part of this staff anymore.

It was one of the most explosive and personal attacks anyone in the division had ever heard—and many of the staff members were on hand to hear the entire exchange. It was especially remarkable that such an emotional outburst occurred in this division. The five staff members of that office are known to be a particularly close-knit group. Individually they are extremely capable, energetic, and highly motivated professionals. Collectively, they are perceived to be among the most congenial, friendly, and productive divisions in the agency.

The luncheon incident was one of many consequences of a series of preceding events. It was important, however, because it made visible an underlying problem in the division that had been masked or quietly discussed behind closed doors. The celebration of each staff member's birthday with a luncheon had become a tradition in the division. It served several purposes, not the least of which were to maintain morale and heighten an "esprit de corps." It was also a means to recognize each person as an individual and to foster the kinship among all that had developed over time.

The two staff members involved, Roger and Catherine, had been good friends for over eight years and had known each other in several professional settings. For the past two years they had been working together in the division as peers. Although a sense of competition could have worked a wedge between their friendship, this had not happened, primarily because they worked in different substantive areas and both received a high level of recognition for their contributions to the division and the agency. This is not to say that the potential for such conflict did not exist. Both had excellent academic and professional credentials and had started with the division on precisely the same date. Although Roger (whose birthday was to be celebrated) was several years older, it was Catherine who had the senior grade and was in fact the Deputy Director of the division.

Roger had recently been elected president of the local union. This was a very demanding position because the agency was currently facing serious labor/management problems. Of necessity, Roger's union activities consumed great portions of his time and much of the work had to be done during duty hours.

Both Roger and Catherine worked for the same immediate supervisor, Joann. Her reputation as a dynamic and capable manager had been the product of a 10-year career with the agency. Now, as a Division Director, she was recognized as one of the agency's most capable and forceful managers. It was also perceived by many that she was "anti-union."

Catherine wanted to get to the bottom of the situation. The day after the blowup, she confronted Roger, as a friend, for an explanation of his peculiar behavior the day before. The discussion went smoothly at first and then turned bitter as the depth of Roger's frustration came out. In confidence, he revealed to Catherine a growing antagonism between himself and Joann on the issue of his ability to perform both the functions of union president and his job. In particular, she just recently assigned another staff member to assist him in one of his major projects because he was "not handling the job as effectively as it needed to be handled." Joann had also openly questioned his ability to give both roles the attention they demanded, and advised him that she felt he was neglecting his work in preference for union activities.

Catherine gets an even bigger earful. Roger was furious that such allegations were being made about his performance. His job performance had never before been challenged in such a manner. In addition, the agency's annual performance review period was scheduled for the near future. He firmly believed he could handle both responsibilities equally, and rejected the notion that one had to be performed at the expense of the other. He also was quite familiar with the legal and procedural safeguards of his position as union president, and did not hesitate to tell Joann he would exert the "power of his office" if her allegations persisted.

At this point, Roger seriously considered bringing charges against her for unfair labor practices. Even if his charges were not successful, the mere issuance of them would besmirch Joann's professional career; her defense against them would also mean personal costs in terms of time and resources.

Although Catherine was certainly sympathetic to Roger's position she could not help but believe there was another side to the story: that of a responsible manager, Joann, who was faced with a delicate situation but who nonetheless wanted to face the challenge directly and establish an equitable resolution before problems became crises. There were many questions involved. Exactly what allowances should be made for an executive officer of the labor union to perform union functions? What percentage of time could be legitimately spent in such activities? What was agency policy on the issue and what did the law require? Since the law does require federal agencies to allow union executives leave time for union activities, are there different standards of performance by which to judge such employees? Is it fair (or even legal) to expect the same productivity and level of workload from employees who also serve as union officials? If not, is the quantity of work expected from the division also judged differently? How is the workforce deficit rectified for the division when union officials conduct union business during their normal duty hours? What remedial action can a division manager take if the staff member's job performance suffers as a result of involvement in union activities?

The answers to these and many other related questions were not obvious, and might come only with difficulty. Past experience with the agency's responses to questions of related seriousness was quite negative. In particular, the Personnel Office as much as refused to set policy in such areas and preferred to deal with individual problems like this one on an ad hoc basis. The agency was even more unresponsive to matters relating to union questions, since the notion of an organized labor force was somewhat new. Agency administrators and managers simply did not know how to respond to such situations and preferred making errors of omission to making errors of commission.

Catherine got the opportunity to hear the other side of the issue later that week. At the conclusion of an afternoon meeting with Joann, the subject came up. It was clear she wanted to discuss it. As Catherine was her deputy and trusted friend, Joann often asked her opinion on various management decisions she faced. Not only did it help her to verbalize the issues, but it was a good source of on-the-job training for her second-in-command.

As the discussion continued, serious implications were raised for the division, the agency, the union, and the individuals involved. One aspect that Catherine had not anticipated, however, was the extent to which Joann had taken the problem personally—she was obviously upset about the situation and felt somewhat victimized by the circumstances in which she found herself. She also expressed a sense of feeling abandoned by upper management, in that they knew of her present problem but offered no guidance or direction.

After most of the elements of the situation were on the table she turned to Catherine and said: "I have never been in such a delicate situation. I am held accountable for the productivity and output of this division. Everyone has to carry their weight here or it will be unfair to all of us. I have to judge each individual's performance equally in terms of both quantity and quality. Do I have to use a different rating scale for one individual? If I do, what is it?

"I tried to talk with Roger about some of these issues, but I just cannot make any headway. He has tuned me out; he does not understand the situation from my perspective and has refused to meet me halfway. The situation is not getting any better, either. I tried to approach him about this as it relates to his ability to perform his job. Both jobs he is trying to do are demanding and require a great deal of attention. I cannot imagine how anyone could perform both jobs adequately unless some compromises are made.

"I think he misunderstood me, because he became enraged and stormed out of my office. We have not spoken to each other since and I refuse to go to him unless he apologizes to me. What should I do?"

∾o∾

INSTRUCTIONS AND QUESTIONS

You are Catherine. You are torn between two strong allegiances—one to your supervisor, who has relied on you in the past and respects your judgment and opinion in such matters; the other to your friend, who has confided in you that the extent of his frustration has reached the point where he is considering bringing charges of unfair labor practice and harassment against your supervisor.

It seems irreconcilable. You realize that the rumors have already leaked out about the problem between Joann and Roger. This could lead to significant problems for Joann and the division if other division heads attempt to use this situation to illustrate her inability as a manager. You would like to warn Joann that she faces possible legal charges and should proceed with caution but feel reluctant to do so, for it would violate a confidence with Roger.

At that moment, Joann takes a phone call and asks to be left alone for a bit, but she adds that it will be brief and she wants to see you in a few minutes to finish the conversation.

1.   What should you do?
2.   If you were Joann, what would you do?

48

One Supervisor's Analysis

Traci Jordan comes to work for the State Revenue Bureau on September 15, 1990, and is assigned to work in the Management Services Division. Her duties are to (1) answer the telephone, (2) photocopy and fax, (3) collect and distribute the mail, (4) serve as microcomputer backup operator, and (4) relieve the division secretary for breaks and lunch.

In addition to the division secretary, there are four management analysts in the bureau: Fred Sims, Hal Davids, Jennie King, and Gail Jenkins. The unit chief is Mac Michaels.

That's me: Mac Michaels. Most people call me "Mike." I'm 48 and I have been in my present job for eight years. I guess I'll be in my present job until I retire. But there are always surprises to keep me interested and on top of my job. I hope never to go stale in my work.

It is not long before the office buzzes with rumors about Traci's "antics." For example, she is said to spend her time at her desk drawing turtles, giving "originals" to people she likes. (I received no turtle.) Also, she "freaks out" over attractive men's ties. On occasion, she supposedly cuts the label from a tie so she can keep it. (She leaves my tie alone.) On one occasion she trades her bra for a tie. She removes the bra without disrobing, in the presence of two male employees of the bureau. I hear about that in a hurry.

So, Traci gets my early attention. I quickly learn that Traci resents having work returned to her if there are errors or if it is not very neat. Traci clearly does not enjoy answering the phone or any other "secretarial duties," for that matter. It also seems she prefers working for the male members of the bureau. As her supervisor, I hold my tongue and attempt to think through Traci's behavior.

Traci is an attractive 20-year-old who is working because her husband is in school. I soon learn that there are some types of work she likes more than others. Traci is good at computer graphics and data base management. Therefore, I begin to let Traci design brochures and prepare reports for the bureau. I also assign her to work directly with Fred Sims and to be trained to operate the Management Information System (MIS) for the bureau.

I soon begin to notice an improvement in Traci's work and her entire attitude. There is less hostility when it is necessary to ask her to redo a report or to "rush" a letter. I also hear less and less about Traci's rumored antics.

I mentally pat myself on the back and definitely arrive at these conclusions about Traci's adjustment problems and the recent changes in her attitude:

- Traci is above average in intelligence.
- She is young and somewhat rebellious; probably had strict parents.
- This job is her first full-time job.
- She is initially bored. She does not consider her original duties meaningful.
- She considers most members of the staff "prudes" and delights in shocking them.
- She is basically a "free spirit" and quite honest.
- The changes I introduce give her more meaningful job duties.
- She is now more confident of herself at work and can get attention by doing a good job on a more meaningful set of tasks.
- Traci now has less need to draw attention to herself.

I tell Traci about my assessment of the situation. She admits that she had tremendous problems with her job at first. She was never given a proper orientation to her job duties, and she tells me I was the bad guy in that aspect of her work. She did not enjoy answering the phone and filling in for the division secretary, stating that these duties were extremely dull.

I learned that Traci was involved in a severe traffic accident at about age 14 or 15. The accident left her mother a cripple, and Traci herself was in a coma for a number of weeks. When she recovered, she could not remember a year and half of her life. Her father is a retired Marine of stoic Pennsylvania Dutch background. She does not like her father or his strictness and bitterly resents the burden of having had to care for her mother for several years until her death from complications as a result of the accident.

After returning to high school, Traci became extremely promiscuous, claiming sex with as many as 25 different men in a month. Of course, she says, she practiced "safe sex." She also became involved with using illegal drugs and, during this period, she reported a number of abortions.

Traci quit school as soon as she was 18. She obtained her high school diploma by taking an equivalency exam, ranking in the 97th percentile. Shortly thereafter Traci married her husband, after a brief period of living together. Traci's only previous work history consisted of summer jobs, then work for a university where she had a great deal of leeway in what she did and when.

Traci disliked her original job because the work was dull and routine and because there was little opportunity to really learn anything about the mission of the organization. She hates to be thought dumb and therefore resents not being adequately trained. She prefers working with men rather than with women. She describes most of the other female employees as "old fogeys" and enjoys saying and doing things that she knows will shock them. It is funny, she reveals, to watch them gossip about her latest activities. This adds color to her workday.

I learn that Traci still has problems with her job, but she does enjoy the extra work. She has begun to take more pride in her work, and its quality improves.

This information really gets me into action. I know what I have to do: I'll keep adding to Traci's job as long as she continues to thrive on the work. I'll make her the best employee in the bureau!

∽०∾

INSTRUCTIONS AND QUESTIONS

You are a friend of Mike's. You share many interests and likes. One day, during lunch, he tells you this story with great attention to detail. When you worked under Mike as an intern, the two of you hit it off in spite of the 10-plus year difference in your ages.

Mike tells you about his diagnosis and plan of action. He is bubbling over with enthusiasm. (You don't even have a chance to tell Mike that you are likely to become his new boss next month.) There are several aspects about what Mike has just told you that bother you. Mike has been a successful supervisor, and you certainly do not want to alienate him. The transition from friend/peer to friend/supervisor will be difficult as it is.

Do you really want your supervisors to get involved the way Mike has with Traci? Some of the history of this situation concerns you and you're not sure you want Traci in the bureau when and if you become Mike's supervisor. What can you do?

Index

The numerals in this topical index are case numbers.

ADA Issues: 9, 12, 29, 32

Authority figures: 10, 12, 17, 35, 38, 44, 45, 46

Bargaining and negotiation: 2, 3, 5, 6, 7, 36, 37, 47

Budgeting: 3, 14, 22, 36, 46

Collaboration: 2, 4, 12, 16, 20, 25, 36

Communications: 4, 13, 15, 17, 22, 24, 25, 30, 35, 37, 38, 40, 42, 45, 47

Community/client relations: 2, 12, 13, 16, 20, 24, 25, 31, 35, 42

Conflict and cooperation: 7, 8, 10, 12, 14, 15, 18, 20, 21, 33, 40, 42, 44, 47

Confrontation or avoidance: 1, 5, 6, 8, 9, 28, 34, 37, 40, 42

Contracting: 8, 14, 18, 22, 36

Costs and benefits: 4, 17, 22, 23, 27, 36

Delegation: 2, 13, 14, 15, 17, 23, 26, 27

Disciplinary action: 5, 7, 8, 17, 33, 40, 41, 42

Employee/labor relations: 1, 5, 6, 7, 26, 31, 45, 46, 47

Equity: 3, 5, 6, 7, 12, 22, 28, 31, 36

Ethical dilemmas: 1, 5, 8, 9, 10, 11, 12, 14, 16, 17, 35, 38, 39, 40

Financial management and planning: 3, 8, 22, 36, 45

First-line supervision: 1, 7, 14, 18, 23, 26, 33, 37, 39, 41, 42, 44, 46

Gender-related issues: 5, 7, 26, 28, 31, 39, 40, 41, 42, 47

Goal setting: 2, 3, 13, 14, 15, 17, 23, 25, 26, 30, 42, 45

Group process: 14, 17, 19, 37, 40, 41, 45

Headquarters/field: 3, 22, 26, 28, 35, 42

Interagency issues: 2, 3, 6, 12, 22, 25, 36, 38

Internships: 6

Interpersonal confrontation: 1, 7, 8, 9, 10, 12, 26, 29, 33, 39, 42, 46, 47

Job assignment: 2, 7, 8, 10, 14, 18, 23, 26, 27, 29, 32, 37, 42, 44, 48

Jurisdiction: 4, 16, 20, 22, 36

Leadership issues: 3, 13, 17, 19, 20, 21, 24, 26, 34, 43, 45, 47

Legal procedures: 4, 7, 8, 10, 12, 29, 35, 41, 47

Lifestyle differences: 12, 15, 20, 29, 33, 44

Line-staff relations: 7, 13, 18, 21, 23, 26, 29, 30, 37

Loyalty: 8, 10, 34

Major personal needs: 1, 15, 32, 34, 40

Managerial style: 1, 5, 13, 14, 15, 17, 18, 21, 26, 30, 39, 42, 43, 44, 46

Mass media: 4, 11, 20, 35, 38

Mental and emotional health: 5, 32, 40, 41, 44

Minority group issues: 11, 28, 31, 42

Motivation and morale: 1, 5, 6, 14, 17, 18, 19, 30, 33, 34, 42, 43, 45, 46

Operations management: 8, 14, 18, 19, 36, 38, 45

Organizational change and culture: 13, 21, 23, 24, 25, 26, 31, 37, 43, 45, 46

Organizational structure: 2, 3, 16, 18, 22, 23, 24, 25, 36, 37, 38

Performance appraisal: 5, 13, 17, 19, 30, 34, 40, 42, 44, 47

Personal dilemmas: 1, 9, 10, 11, 12, 13, 15, 17, 19, 28, 31, 34, 35, 38, 47, 48

Personnel actions: 5, 6, 7, 19, 26, 27, 28, 29, 30, 31, 32, 33, 37, 39, 40, 41

Planning: 2, 3, 4, 13, 17, 19

Policies and procedures: 1, 4, 6, 7, 8, 11, 23, 30, 34, 35, 37, 38, 39, 44, 46

Politics and administration: 3, 4, 6, 9, 11, 13, 16, 20, 22, 24, 25, 28, 35, 38

Professionals: 1, 2, 6, 7, 12, 14, 17, 21, 26, 37, 45

Program evaluation: 8, 13, 22, 34, 38

Program or management analysis: 2, 4, 5, 6, 8, 13, 17, 18, 22, 23, 36

Quality of work life: 15, 23, 43

Reorganization: 3, 13, 15, 18, 19, 21, 22, 23, 24, 25, 26

Resistance to change: 7, 18, 21, 23, 26, 33, 34, 42, 43, 46

Sexual conduct: 29, 33, 40, 41, 44

Social problems: 9, 11, 12, 20, 24, 27, 28, 29, 30, 31, 32, 34, 36, 42, 44, 46

Status: 7, 26, 42

Succession: 14, 18, 21, 34
Supporting staff: 1, 8, 18, 30, 39, 41, 42, 43
Supporting supervisors: 5, 6, 7, 10, 13, 34, 47
Total Quality Management: 8, 18, 21, 22, 23, 33, 37
Training: 5, 7, 9, 14, 19, 23, 26, 27, 29, 33, 41, 44
Value differences: 9, 11, 12, 20, 24, 26, 28, 29, 33, 34, 40, 42, 45, 48
Work-family interface: 15, 17, 27, 30, 39, 40

CASES IN PUBLIC MANAGEMENT
Fifth Edition
Edited by John Beasley
Production supervision by Kim Vander Steen
Cover design by Lesiak/Crampton Design, Park Ridge, Illinois
Composition by Point West, Inc., Carol Stream, Illinois
Paper, Finch Opaque
Printed and bound by McNaughton & Gunn, Saline, Michigan